Finance Bill 2020

&

Vivad se Vishwaas Scheme 2020

Made Easy

Mayank Mohanka

FCA, B.Com(Hons)SRCC

1

ISBN 9781648283901

Acknowledgement

Any good piece of 'book-writing-work' not only requires the skills, passion, dedication and perseverance of the author but also involves the selfless and invaluable contribution of many others who are directly or indirectly connected with him/her.

In my case also, this present piece of 'book-writing-work' has become possible and has seen the light of the day only because of the selfless contribution and invaluable support, guidance and blessings of some very dear and special people in my life.

My 'soul-mate - my wife Sonia' and 'my soul - my little son Dhruv' are the first ones who deserve every bit of my gratitude, love, affection and acknowledgement and I owe to them every single second of my personal time which I spent on penning down this piece of writing and not with them. It was their patience, encouragement, unconditional love and invaluable support that motivated me and allowed me to go ahead with this noble pursuit.

I also owe my sincere gratitude to my Parents who have always selflessly and lovingly showered and blessed me with all their love, support and guidance through-out.

My mentors Sh. K.C. Jain & Sh. Sushil Kumar Jain also deserves every bit of my respect, admiration and affection as their selfless love, support and blessings have made me a more capable and better person in my life.

My team-mates Ms. Nancy Tayal, CA & Ms. Akanksha Arora, CA also deserve a special mention here because of their invaluable support and precious inputs in penning down this Book.

I also owe my sincere gratitude, respect and acknowledgement to the Notion Press Publication, for giving me such a nice and reputed self-publication platform to showcase my writing skills.

Most importantly, I thank and pray the Almighty who have always blessed me with physical and mental well-being and have always shown me the right path in my life.

Warm Regards

Mayank Mohanka

Preface

This Book "Finance Bill 2020 & Vivad se Vishwaas Bill 2020 Made Easy" is a ready referencer and a practical guide for understanding and learning all the amendments and provisions of the Finance Bill 2020 and Vivad se Vishwas Bill 2020.

As per nature's law, human memory is conditioned to understand and memorise those things, faster and better, which eyes see and ears hear and the same is applicable to budget announcements also.

Most often, the amendments which are covered in the budget speech of the Finance Minister attract all the lime-light of TV channels and news-paper headlines and the resultant focus and attention of general public at large and in the process some very crucial and significant nuances and nitty-gritties of budget amendments get remain unnoticed.

The idea of this Book was coined by my father Sh. S.K. Mohanka, who is himself a seasoned chartered accountant. His sound advise of reading and understanding carefully 'in-between-the lines' provisions in the Finance Bill has been instrumental in penning down this piece of writing.

I have always believed that,

"Beauty & Devil Both Lie in the Details."

This Book decodes in detail the carefully and deeply knitted and worded nuances of the legislative amendments and new insertions, in the Finance Bill 2020, and Vivad se Vishwas Bill 2020, in an easy to understand, comprehensible and simple manner with practical illustrations.

Kew Highlights of the BOOK

- *Break-Even Point Analysis between the Old & New Personal Taxation Regime.*
- *Detailed Analysis as to When the New Personal Tax Regime u/s 115BAC will be beneficial vis-à-vis Old Regime.*
- *Detailed Analysis of 'Vivad se Vishwas Scheme 2020' and decoding all its nuances and practicalities.*
- *Detailed Analysis of All the Proposed Amendments and Provisions in Finance Bill 2020, concerning Start-Ups.*
- *Detailed Analysis of Proposed Amendments and Provisions in Finance Bill 2020, concerning Charitable Trusts, Educational Institutions & Hospitals.*
- *Detailed Analysis of the Impact Assessment of Removal of Dividend Distribution Tax.*
- *Detailed Analysis of New TDS Provisions for E-Commerce Transactions.*

- *Detailed Analysis of New Penalty Provisions for False/Bogus Entries.*
- *Detailed Analysis of International Taxation Provisions and Amendments proposed in Finance Bill 2020.*
- *Detailed Analysis of New Tax Audit Limits*
- *Detailed Analysis of Amendments concerning Resident Co-operative Societies.*
- *Detailed Analysis of Provisions concerning Faceless e-Appeals & e-Penalty.*

'Learning and improving is a continuous process' and so honest and valuable suggestions and feedback are invited and solicited from the *'worthy readers'*, at my email id **mayankmohanka@gmail.com** for further improvement.

"व्यये कृते वर्धते नित्यं। विद्या धनं सर्वे धनं प्रधानम्।।"

Knowledge multiplies manifold by sharing. It is a supreme form of wealth.

Warm Regards

Mayank Mohanka

About the Author

Sh. Mayank Mohanka, is a seasoned Tax Practitioner, a Fellow Member of the Institute of Chartered Accountants of India and a Bachelor of Commerce, in Honours Degree from Shree Ram College of Commerce (SRCC), Delhi University. He is a Senior Partner in a New Delhi based established and reputed CA Firm, M/s Sushil Jeetpuria & Company.

He has a 15+ years of rich and profound experience in the field of Taxation (Direct & Indirect), and Advisory. He makes Representations for a widely diversified cross section of industries including Power Sector, Banking & Finance, Real Estate, Food Processing, Infrastructure, Manufacturing,

Education and Information Technology, before Authority for Advance Rulings, ITAT, Education Boards and other appropriate forums.

He has to his credit 40 distinguished, informative, useful and practically oriented published articles in reputed journals, sites and platforms including Taxmann, on wide ranging subjects including Income Tax, GST, PF, ESI, IBC, Corporate Laws, Education Acts & FEMA.

He has also authored a 'Best Seller' Professional Book titled *"Guide to e-Assessment with Real-Time Case Studies & Suggestive e-Submissions"*, with Taxmann Publications, on the New Faceless Income-tax e-Assessments in India and the Book *'SUPER 21'* with Notion Press, treasuring his real-life winning representations on Income Tax, GST, PF, ESI, IBC & Banking Regulation Act, in his professional practice.

INDEX

Chapter 1

Decoding the Lesser Known Nuances of Finance Bill 2020

The Hon'ble FM Smt. Nirmala Sitharaman has commenced her Budget Speech concerning the Direct Tax Proposals, while presenting the Finance Bill 2020, in the Parliament, on 1.2.2020, by quoting a verse from 'Raghuvamsa' by Kalidas, which reads as under:

"प्रजानामेवभूत्यर्थंसताभ्योबलिमग्रहीत्।
सहस्रगुणमुत्स्रष्टुमादत्तेहिरसंरविः ॥"

Surya, the Sun, collects vapour from little drops of water. So does the King. They give back copiously. They collect only for people's wellbeing. **[Verse 18, Sarga 1 Raghuvamsa by Kalidasa]**

Well, the first prima-facie impression and euphoria of the Union Budget 2020, especially the Finance Bill 2020, appeared to be one of a taxpayer-pro budget, with the Queen (Read FM), giving copiously to her masses.

But is this euphoria for a real?

As per nature's law, human memory is conditioned to understand and memorise those things, faster and better, which eyes see and ears hear and the same is applicable to budget announcements also.

Most often, the amendments which are covered in the budget speech of the Finance Minister attract all the lime-light of TV channels and news-paper headlines and the resultant focus and attention of general public at large and in the process some very crucial and significant nuances and nitty-gritties of budget amendments get remain unnoticed.

I have always believed that,

"Beauty & Devil Both Lie in the Details."

So, let us put on our analytical skills at work and decode the very carefully and deeply knitted and worded nuances of the legislative amendments and new insertions, as proposed in the Finance Bill 2020.

1.1 The Key Amendments in Income Tax Act, Proposed by Finance Bill 2020, at a Glance

1. New Regime of Personal Taxes with Reduced Tax Rates and No Deductions

The Finance Bill 2020 has proposed to provide an option to individual and Hindu Undivided Family (HUF) assessees, to be taxed at following lower rates if they do not avail the specified deductions.

Total Income (Rs)	Rate (%)
Up to 2,50,000	Nil
From 2,50,001 to 5,00,000	5
From 5,00,001 to 7,50,000	10
From 7,50,001 to 10,00,000	15
From 10,00,001 to 12,50,000	20
From 12,50,001 to 15,00,000	25
Above 15,00,000	30

Surcharge and cess shall be continued to be levied at the existing rates.

2. Vivad se Vishwaas Scheme 2020

It has been proposed to bring out a scheme for reducing the direct tax litigation. Taxpayers in whose case appeals are pending at any level can take the benefit from this scheme. Under the scheme, taxpayer would be required to pay only the amount of the disputed taxes and there will be complete waiver of interest and penalty provided they make payment by 31st March, 2020. For disputed penalty, interest and fee not connected with the disputed tax, the taxpayer would be required to pay only 25% of the same for settling the dispute. A tax payer shall be required to pay 110% of the disputed tax (the excess 10% shall be limited to the amount of related penalty and interest, if any) and 30% of penalty, interest and fee in case of payment after 31st March, 2020.

3. Restriction on Powers of ITAT to Grant Stay of Demand

The Finance Bill 2020 has proposed to make it mandatory for the assessees to deposit atleast 20% of their outstanding income-tax demand, so as to make them eligible to file their application for stay of demand before the ITAT.

4. Penalty for False/Bogus Entries

To discourage taxpayers to manipulate their books of accounts by recording false entries including fake invoices to claim wrong input credit in GST, it has been proposed to provide for penalty for these malpractices.

It has been proposed in the Finance Bill 2020, to levy a penalty on an assessee equivalent to the amount of false/bogus entries in his Books of Accounts by inserting a new section 271AAD.

5. Tightening of Provisions concerning Registration and Exemption of Charitable Trusts, Educational Institutions & Hospitals

It has been proposed in the Finance Bill 2020 that all the existing charitable trusts, educational institutions and hospitals have to compulsorily apply afresh for their registration under the Income Tax Act and registration so granted shall be valid only for a period of 5 years. Thus, now all such organisations and institutions have to apply for renewal of their registration under the Income Tax Act, after every five years. The similar provisions are also applicable to all new organisations and institutions making application for their registration for the first time.

It is also proposed to provide filing of statement of donation by donee so that the deduction claimed by the donor in its tax return can be pre-filled.

6. Digital Transformation of Indian Tax Administration

a. Faceless e-Appeals & e-Penalty

In order to impart greater efficiency, transparency and accountability to the assessment process, a new faceless assessment scheme has already been introduced. In order to ensure that the reforms initiated by the Income Tax Department to eliminate human interface from the system reach the next level, it is proposed to provide enabling power for launching of Faceless appeal on the lines of Faceless assessment.

The Finance Bill 2020 has inserted enabling provisions in the Act, so as to facilitate the incorporation of the new schemes of faceless e-appeals and faceless e-penalty, to be notified in near future, on similar lines of the already notified 'faceless e-assessment scheme 2019.

b. Modification in the scope of faceless e-assessment

It is proposed to widen the scope of faceless assessment scheme to cover those cases in which assessment is being completed *ex-parte*.

7. Safe Harbour Limit u/s 43CA, 50C & 56 of the Act

The safe harbour limit u/s 43CA, 50C and 56 of the Income tax Act concerning stamp duty valuation based on circle rates in cases of sale or transfer of land, building and house properties has been increased from the existing 5% to 10%.

It has also been proposed to clarify that in case of a capital asset, being land or building or both, the fair market value of such an asset on 1st day of April, 2001 shall not exceed the stamp duty value of such asset as on 1st day of April, 2001, where such stamp duty value is available.

8. Incentives to Start-Ups

In order to encourage the start-ups to employ highly talented employees at a relatively low salary by granting them Employee Stock Option Plan (ESOPs), it has been proposed to defer the tax payment on these ESOPs granted by start-up to their employees by five years or till the employee leaves the company or when the said employee sells those shares, whichever is earliest.

Further, in order to extend benefit of tax holiday to larger start-ups, it is proposed to increase the turnover threshold for claiming tax holiday from existing Rs. 25 crores to Rs. 100 crores. Further, in order to address the concerns of start-ups which may not have adequate profit in initial years for availing this holiday, it is proposed to extend the period of eligibility for claim of 100% deduction from the existing 7 years to 10 years.

9. Removal of Dividend Distribution Tax

At present dividend is taxed in the hands of company distributing such dividend. It has been proposed to shift to classical system of taxing dividend in the hands of shareholders.

10. Raising of limit for Tax Audit u/s 44AB

In order to help small and medium enterprises, it has been proposed to raise the turnover threshold for compulsory tax audit from existing Rs. 1 crore to Rs. 5 crores in a case where cash receipt is not more than 5% of total receipt and cash payment is not more than 5% of total payment. Further, in order to reduce the compliance cost, it is also proposed to provide that tax audit report to be filed a month before the due date of filing income- tax return. Accordingly, the said due date for filing of income-tax returns is proposed to be changed from 30th September to 31st October of the relevant assessment year so that there is no change in the date of finalisation of tax audit.

11. TDS on E-commerce transactions

In order to widen and deepen the tax net, it has been proposed to provide that e-commerce operator shall deduct TDS on all payments or credits to e-commerce participants at the rate of 1% in PAN/Aadhaar cases and 5% in non-PAN/Aadhaar cases. In order to provide relief to small businessman, it is proposed to provide exemption to an individual and HUF who receives less than Rs. 5 lakh and furnishes PAN/Aadhaar.

12. Limit on Exemption of Employer's contribution to certain funds

It has been proposed to put an upper cap of seven lakh and fifty thousand rupees in a year on tax exempt employer's contribution in recognized provident fund, superannuation fund and NPS in the accounts of an employee.

13. Relief and simplification for Co-operative Societies

In order to provide relief and simplify the taxation regime, it is proposed to provide an option to cooperative societies to be taxed at 22% plus 10% surcharge plus 4% cess, if they do not avail certain specified deduction/exemption. Further, it is also proposed to exempt these cooperative societies from Alternative Minimum Tax (AMT).

14. Withdrawal of Exemption available to UPSC Chairman & Members & Chief Election Commissioner & Election Commissioners

The Finance Bill 2020 has proposed to withdraw certain exemptions available to UPSC Chairman & Members & Chief Election Commissioner & Election Commissioners, and bring them in the income tax net.

It is proposed to withdraw the exemption on certain perquisites and allowances provided to Chairman and members of Union Public Service Commission and to Chief Election Commissioner and Election Commissioners.

15. International Taxation

a. Widening the scope of Safe Harbour Rules and Advance Pricing Agreement

In order to provide tax certainty to taxpayers in the matter of attribution of profit to permanent establishment (PE), it is proposed to widen the scope of Advanced Pricing Agreement (APA) and Safe Harbour Regime (SHR), by providing that determination of attribution of profit to PE shall also be in the scope of SHR and APA.

b. Exempting Non-Residents from filing of Income-tax return on certain conditions

In order to reduce compliance burden of non-residents, it has been proposed to exempt them from filing income-tax return on their income of the nature of royalty or fee for technical services, if tax has been deducted at the rate given in section 115A.

c. Alignment of MLI to DTAA

It has been proposed to amend the provision allowing India to enter into Double Taxation

Avoidance Agreements (DTAA) with other countries or territories or association, to align with the new preamble mandated by Multilateral Convention to Implement Tax Treaty Related Measures to Prevent Base Erosion and Profit Shifting (commonly referred to as MLI), as India has already ratified MLI.

d. Deferment of Significant Economic Presence (SEP)

It is proposed to defer the enactment of Significant Economic Presence (SEP) to Financial Year 2021-22 as G-20 OECD report on digital economy is expected by that time. It is also proposed to provide for source rule for revenue from advertisement targeted to India customers and revenue from sale of Indian sourced data.

e. Foreign Portfolio Investors

It is proposed to align exemption from the provision of indirect transfer to Foreign Portfolio Investors in line with new SEBI FPI regulations. It is also proposed to rationalise the definition of royalty.

16. Reduction in Period of Stay in India for Residential Status

It has been proposed to reduce the time of stay in India from 182 days to 120 days for an Indian citizen or person of Indian origin to become resident in India. Consequently, it is proposed to relax the provision of "resident but not ordinarily resident" so that a resident who has been non-resident in seven out of ten previous years would be resident but not ordinarily resident. It is also proposed to provide that an Indian citizen who is not liable to tax anywhere would be deemed to be resident in India.

17. Widening the scope of Dispute Resolution Panel (DRP)

It has been proposed to widen the scope of references to DRP by including all non-residents as eligible assessee and to clarify that all variation which are prejudicial to the assessee shall be within the scope of DRP.

18. Taxpayer's Charter

With the objective of enhancing the efficiency of the delivery system of the Income Tax Department, it is proposed to provide that the CBDT shall adopt a Taxpayer's Charter and issue necessary direction for the implementation of the Charter.

19. Check on Survey Powers

To increase transparency in survey operation, it is proposed to provide that if the survey is not based on information provided by prescribed authority, then approval of Commissioner or Principal Commissioner of Income-tax is required.

20. Enlargement in the Scope of Authorised Person for Verification of ITRs and for Appearance as Authorised Representatives

It is proposed to authorise Board to prescribe person who can verify the return of income in the cases of a company and a limited liability partnership. It is also proposed to authorise Board to prescribe person who can appear as an authorised representative.

This will help companies under Insolvency proceedings and in liquidation. It is also proposed to align the due date of Partner and Firm.

In the ensuing Chapters, we shall be learning and understanding in detail, all the nuances, practicalities and nitty-gritties of all these proposed amendments and new insertions in the Finance Bill 2020.

Chapter 2

New Personal Tax Regime u/s 115BAC

2.1 Incorporation of New Personal Taxation Regime of Reduced Tax Rates with No Deductions in Case of Individuals & HUFs (applicable w.e.f. AY 2021-22).

It is a fundamental principle of any economy that for the revival and acceleration of its slowing growth rate, increase in consumption levels is a sine-qua-non. For increasing consumption levels, increase in personal disposable income is essential. So, to put the wheels of economy back on track, at the dawn of Budget Day on 1.2.2020, there was a tremendous pressure on and expectations from the Finance Minister Smt. Nirmala Sitharaman, to reduce the personal tax rates in the Finance Bill 2020.

In line with the new regime of reduced corporate tax rates, introduced by the Taxation Laws (Amendment) Act 2019, the Finance Bill 2020, has proposed the **insertion of a new section 115BAC**, providing for a new personal taxation regime in the cases of individuals and HUFs (hereinafter referred to as 'assessees'), wherein the 'assessees' have been given the option to either continue with the existing personal tax rates with availment of full specified deductions, or to opt for the new regime of reduced personal tax rates with restrictions on approximately 70% of the specified deductions, currently available to them under different chapters and sections.

2.2 New Personal Tax Slabs

The newly proposed reduced personal tax rates in the case of individuals & HUFs u/s 115BAC, in the Finance Bill 2020, applicable w.e.f. AY 2021-22, are as under:

Total Income (Rs)	New Regime Tax Rate (%)	Old Regime Tax Rate (%)
Up to 2,50,000	Nil	Nil
From 2,50,001 to 5,00,000	5	5
From 5,00,001 to 7,50,000	10	20
From 7,50,001 to 10,00,000	15	20
From 10,00,001 to 12,50,000	20	30
From 12,50,001 to 15,00,000	25	30
Above 15,00,000	30	30

Surcharge and cess shall be continued to be levied at the existing rates.

2.3 'Specified Deductions' Not Allowed under New Personal Tax Regime of Reduced Taxes:

In order to avail the benefit of reduced tax rates u/s 115BAC, an individual/HUF assessee has to forgo the 'specified deductions' available to him under various chapters and sections of the Income Tax Act.

So, there is a big catch to this prima-facie 'assessee-beneficial' regime, and that is the restriction/denial of the most common and recurring deductions like deductions u/s 80C, 80CCD, 80D, HRA, LTA, Standard Deduction, interest on self-occupied/let out property, to name a few.

To be more specific, an individual or HUF opting for the new taxation regime under the newly inserted section 115BAC of the Act shall not be entitled to the following exemptions/ deductions (hereinafter referred to as the **"specified deductions"**):

(i) Leave travel concession as contained in clause (5) of section 10;

(ii) House rent allowance as contained in clause (13A) of section 10;

(iii) Some of the allowance as contained in clause (14) of section 10;

(iv) Allowances to MPs/MLAs as contained in clause (17) of section 10;

(v) Allowance for income of minor as contained in clause (32) of section 10;

(vi) Exemption for SEZ unit contained in section 10AA;

(vii) Standard deduction, deduction for entertainment allowance and employment/professional tax as contained in section 16;

(viii) Interest under section 24 in respect of self-occupied or vacant property referred to in sub-section (2) of section 23. (Loss under the head income from house property for rented house shall not be allowed to be set off under any other head and would be allowed to be carried forward as per extant law);

(ix) Additional deprecation under clause (iia) of sub-section (1) of section 32;

(x) Deductions under section 32AD, 33AB, 33ABA;

(xi) Various deduction for donation for or expenditure on scientific research contained in sub-clause (ii) or sub-clause (iia) or sub-clause (iii) of sub-section (1) or sub-section (2AA) of section 35;

(xii) Deduction under section 35AD or section 35CCC;

(xiii) Deduction from family pension under clause (iia) of section 57;

(xiv) Any deduction under chapter VIA (like section 80C, 80CCC, 80CCD, 80D, 80DD, 80DDB, 80E, 80EE, 80EEA, 80EEB, 80G, 80GG, 80GGA, 80GGC, 80IA, 80-IAB, 80-IAC, 80-IB, 80-IBA, etc). However, deduction under sub-section (2) of section 80CCD (employer contribution on account of employee in notified pension scheme) and section 80JJAA (for new employment) can be claimed.

For ready reference and benefit of the worthy readers, the maximum permissible amounts of the above mentioned "specified deductions", which are available to an individual/HUF assessee, under various sections, and which are required to be forgone, in order to avail the benefit of reduced taxation u/s 115BAC, have been tabulated as under:

S. No.	Deduction	Remarks	Available to
1	Leave Travel Concessio n u/s 10(5)	The value of any travel concession or assistance received or due.	Salaried Individual
2	House Rent Allowance u/s 10(13A)	Least of: a. Actual HRA received; b. 50% of [basic salary + DA] for those living in metro cities (40% for non-metros); or c. Actual rent paid less 10% of basic salary + DA	Salaried Individual
3	Other Allowance s u/s 10(14)	Actual amount of such Allowance received	Salaried Individual

4	Allowance s to MPs/MLA s u/s 10(17)	Actual amount of such Allowance received	Salaried Individual
5	Allowance for income of minor u/s 10(32)	Rs.1,500/- per child	Individual
6	Standard Deduction u/s 16	Rs.50,000/-	Salaried Individual
7	Interest u/s 24 in respect of self-occupied or vacant property	Rs.200000/-	Individual /HUF
8	Additional Depreciati on u/s 32(1)(iia)	Allowed to eligible assessee: 20% of the actual cost of Plant and Machinery(35% in case of Notified Backward Areas)	Individual /HUF
9	Deduction from family pension u/s 57(iia)	Least of: One-third of such income or Rs.15,000/-	Individual
10	Any deduction under chapter VI-A (deduction u/s 80CCD(2) and 80JJAA are allowable in both the Regimes):-		
a.	80C, 80CCC, 80CCD(1): For investment	Rs.1,50,000/-	Individual /HUF

	s in specified schemes		
b.	80CCD(1B): Deduction for the deposit under NPS	Rs.50,000/-	Individual
c.	80D: Amount invested in Health Insurance	Rs.25000/- for self, spouse and dependent children;	Individual /HUF
		Rs.25,000/- for parents (Rs.50,000/- if parents are Senior citizen/ Very Senior Citizen);	
		Rs.5,000/- for preventive health check-up of self, spouse, dependent children, father and mother; and	
		Rs.50,000/- for Medical Expenditures on the health of a super senior citizen if Medi-claim insurance is not paid on the health of such person.	
d.	Section 80DD: Expenditure incurred for the medical	Rs.75,000 (Rs.1,25,000 in case of severe disability)	Individual /HUF

	treatment of a dependent		
e.	Section 80DDB: Expenditure incurred for medical treatment of specified diseases	Up to Rs.40,000/- and Rs.1,00,000/- for Senior/ Very Senior Citizen	Individual
f.	Section 80E: Interest paid on Educational Loan	The amount of interest paid during initial year and 7 immediately succeeding assessment years	Individual
g.	Section 80G: Deduction for donations to certain funds, charitable institutions, etc.	Deduction up to 100%/50% of the aggregate amount of donation	Individual /HUF
h.	Section 80GG: Rent paid for residential	Least of the following: a) Rent paid in excess of 10% of total income; b) 25% of the Total Income; or	Individuals not receiving HRA

	accommod ation	c) Rs.5,000/- per month.	
i.	Section 80QQB: Royalty income of books	Least of the following:	Individual
		a) In case of Lump sum payment - maximum of Rs.3,00,000/-	
		b) In other cases - amount of such income subject to maximum of 15% of value of books sold during the previous year.	
j.	Section 80RRB: Royalty of patents	Rs.3,00,000/-	Individual
k.	Section 80TTA: Interest on Savings Bank accounts	Rs.10,000/-	Individual /HUF
l.	Section 80 TTB: Interest on deposits with Post Offices, Banks, Co-operative banks	Rs.50,000/-	Senior and Super Senior Resident Individual s
m.	Section 80U: Persons with Disability	Rs.75,000/- (Rs.1,25,000/- in case of severe disability)	Individual

11	Exemption for SEZ unit u/s 10AA	Deduction to eligible persons as per the provisions of said section.	Individual /HUF
12	Deductions u/s 32AD, 33AB, 33ABA	Deduction to eligible persons as per the provisions of said section.	Individual /HUF
13	Deduction for donation or expenditure on scientific research u/s 35(1)(ii)/(iia)/(iii) or sec 35(2AA)	Deduction to eligible persons as per the provisions of said section.	Individual /HUF
14	Deduction u/s 35AD or section 35CCC	Deduction to eligible persons as per the provisions of said section.	Individual /HUF

It has also been proposed to amend rule 3 of the Rules subsequently, so as to remove exemption in respect of free food and beverage through vouchers provided to the employee, being the person exercising option under the proposed section, by the employer.

2.4 The undermentioned Allowances u/s 10(14) of the Income Tax Act, will continue to remain allowable even under the New Regime of Personal Taxation.

(a) Transport Allowance granted to a divyang employee to meet expenditure for the purpose of commuting between place of residence and place of duty

(b) Conveyance Allowance granted to meet the expenditure on conveyance in performance of duties of an office;

(c) Any Allowance granted to meet the cost of travel on tour or on transfer;

(d) Daily Allowance to meet the ordinary daily charges incurred by an employee on account of absence from his normal place of duty.

This amendment will take effect from 1st April, 2021 and will, accordingly, apply in relation to the AY 2021-22 and subsequent assessment years.

The primary reason for introduction of this new personal taxation regime u/s 115BAC, as intended, has been to be simplification of tax laws, however, ironically, during the transition phase, it is resulting in more complicated scenarios, wherein, the individual and HUF assessees are faced with the difficult and intriguing question and choice of opting for one of the two personal taxation regimes, in order to optimise their taxes.

Therefore, with a view to simplify this complication, a comprehensive *'BREAK-EVEN POINT ANALYSIS',* has been done in ensuing paragraphs, so as to guide and assist the worthy readers, in making good and informative choice and decision of opting for their most optimum tax regimes.

2.4 Break- Even Point Analysis between New & Old Personal Tax Regime

The Break-Even Point i.e. the point where both the new regime of reduced tax rates with no 'specified deductions' and the old regime of increased tax rates with 'specified deductions', for all the Income Levels/ Ranges, have been tabulated in **Master Table I** and have been computed in **Tables 1, 2, 3 4 & 5,** below, for ready reference and benefit of the worthy readers.

Break-Even Point in Terms of 'Specified Deductions'

Usually an individual/HUF assessee has a fair bit of idea about his income range or level. So, at a particular income level, he is faced with the choice of deciding either to avail the 'specified deductions' by making investments etc under various sections like 80C, 80CCC, 80CCD in Chapter VIA, to name a few, under the old tax regime or to forgo the specified deductions, to avail the benefit of reduced tax rates u/s 115BAC under the new regime.

For ready reference and the benefit of the worthy readers, the break-even point in terms of 'specified deductions', at different levels of 'income' have been tabulated in Master Table I, based on detailed computations in Tables 1, 2, 3, 4 & 5, below.

As a thumb rule, the Individuals/HUFs (assessees), having the undermentioned annual incomes will benefit from the new personal tax regime of reduced tax rates u/s 115BAC, only if they are availing 'specified deductions' either less than or equal to the 'specified deductions' at the 'highlighted break-even point' in the below Tables.

However, if the assesses are availing more 'specified deductions', than those at the break-even point, then they will benefit more in the old regime,

of increased tax rates, in terms of their nett. tax outflows.

2.4.1 MASTER TABLE I

Income (INR)	Break Even Point For 'Specified Deductions' (INR)	When is New Tax Regime Beneficial?	When is Old Tax Regime Beneficial?
Up to 500000	0	At Par	At Par
550000	25000	If Deductions are less than or equal to Rs 25000.	If Deductions are more than Rs 25000
600000	50000	If Deductions are less than or equal to Rs 50000.	If Deductions are more than Rs 50000.
650000	75000	If Deductions are less than or equal to Rs 75000.	If Deductions are more than Rs 75000.

Income (INR)	Break Even Point For 'Specified Deductions' (INR)	When is New Tax Regime Beneficial?	When is Old Tax Regime Beneficial?
700000	100000	If Deductions are less than or equal to Rs 100000.	If Deductions are more than Rs 100000.
750000	125000	If Deductions are less than or equal to Rs 125000.	If Deductions are more than Rs 125000.
800000	137500	If Deductions are less than or equal to Rs 137500.	If Deductions are more than Rs 137500.
850000	150000	If Deductions are less than or equal to Rs 150000.	If Deductions are more than Rs 150000.
900000	162500	If Deductions are less than or	If Deductions are more

Income (INR)	Break Even Point For 'Specified Deductions' (INR)	When is New Tax Regime Beneficial?	When is Old Tax Regime Beneficial?
		equal to Rs 162500.	than Rs 162500.
950000	175000	If Deductions are less than or equal to Rs 175000.	If Deductions are more than Rs 175000.
1000000	187500	If Deductions are less than or equal to Rs 187500.	If Deductions are more than Rs 187500.
1050000	187500	If Deductions are less than or equal to Rs 187500.	If Deductions are more than Rs 187500.
1100000	187500	If Deductions are less than or equal to Rs 187500.	If Deductions are more than Rs 187500.

Income (INR)	Break Even Point For 'Specified Deductions' (INR)	When is New Tax Regime Beneficial?	When is Old Tax Regime Beneficial?
1150000	187500	If Deductions are less than or equal to Rs 187500.	If Deductions are more than Rs 187500.
1200000	191670	If Deductions are less than or equal to Rs 191670.	If Deductions are more than Rs 191670.
1250000	208330	If Deductions are less than or equal to Rs 208330.	If Deductions are more than Rs 208330.
1300000	216665	If Deductions are less than or equal to Rs 216665.	If Deductions are more than Rs 216665.
1350000	225000	If Deductions are less than or	If Deductions are more

Income (INR)	Break Even Point For 'Specified Deductions' (INR)	When is New Tax Regime Beneficial?	When is Old Tax Regime Beneficial?
		equal to Rs 225000.	than Rs 225000.
1400000	233330	If Deductions are less than or equal to Rs 233330.	If Deductions are more than Rs 233330.
1450000	241670	If Deductions are less than or equal to Rs 241670.	If Deductions are more than Rs 241670.
1500000 & Above	250000	If Deductions are less than or equal to Rs 250000.	If Deductions are more than Rs 250000.

2.4.1a TABLE 1: Annual Income Range of Rs. 5 lakhs to Rs 7.5 lakhs

A Comparative Analysis between the New and Old Personal Tax Regime, for the Income Range of Rs. 5 lakhs to Rs 7.5 lakhs, has been tabulated below.

Income (INR)	Tax Liability under New Regime (INR)	Amount of Deductions (INR) At Break Even Point					
		0	25000	50000	75000	100000	125000
		Tax Liability under the Old Regime (INR)					
Uptill 500000	0	0	0	0	0	0	0
550000	18200	23400	18200	0	0	0	0
600000	23400	33800	28600	23400	18200	0	0
650000	28600	44200	39000	33800	28600	23400	18200
700000	33800	54600	49400	44200	39000	33800	28600
750000	39000	65000	59800	54600	49400	44200	39000

As can be seen from above table, that an individual or HUF having an annual income of up to Rs. 5 lakhs, will be at par in both the regimes.

An individual/HUF having an annual income of Rs. 5.5 lakhs will benefit from the new regime of reduced personal tax rates only if he is availing the "specified deductions" of less than or equal to Rs. 25,000/-, in a financial year.

However, if the amount of the "specified deductions" available to him is in excess of Rs. 25,000/-, then the assessee will benefit more by continuing with the old personal tax regime, as his tax outflows will be less as compared to the new regime.

So, an individual/HUF assessee, having an annual income of Rs. 5.5 lakhs, will *'break-even'* or will be *'at par'* between the new and old personal tax regime, if he is availing 'specified deductions' of Rs. 25,000/- in a financial year.

Uptill this break-even point in terms of 'specified deductions', he will benefit more in new tax regime

44

and beyond this break-even point, he will benefit more in old tax regime.

Similarly, an individual/HUF assessee, having an annual income of Rs. 6/6.5/7/7.5 lakhs respectively,

will benefit from the new regime of reduced personal tax rates only if he is availing the "specified deductions" of less than or equal to Rs. 0.5/0.75/1/1.25 lakhs respectively/-.

So, the break-even points in terms of 'specified deductions', for an individual/HUF assessee having an annual income of Rs. 6/6.5/7/7.5 lakhs respectively, are Rs. 0.5/0.75/1/1.25 lakhs respectively/-, in a financial year.

Similarly, the break-even points in terms of 'specified deductions', for an individual/HUF assessee having annual income ranging from Rs. 8 lakhs to 15 lakhs and above, have been computed and tabulated in Tables 2, 3, 4 & 5, as under:

2.4.1b TABLE 2: Annual Income Range of Rs. 8 lakhs to Rs 10 lakhs

Income (INR)	Tax Liability under New Regime (INR)	Amount of Deductions (INR) At Break Even Point				
		137500	150000	162500	175000	187500
		Tax Liability under the Old Regime (INR)				
800000	46800	46800	44200	41600	39000	36400
850000	54600	57200	54600	52000	49400	46800
900000	62400	67600	65000	62400	59800	57200
950000	70200	78000	75400	72800	70200	67600
1000000	78000	88400	85800	83200	80600	78000

2.4.1c TABLE 3: Annual Income Range of Rs. 10 lakhs to Rs 12.5 lakhs

Income (INR)	Tax Liability under New Regime - Without any deductions (INR)	Amount of Deductions (INR) At Break Point			
		187500	191670	208332	216665
		Tax Liability under the Old Regime (INR)			
1000000	78000	78000	77133	73667	71934
1050000	88400	88400	87533	84067	82334
1100000	98800	98800	97933	94467	92734
1150000	109200	109200	108333	104867	103134
1200000	119600	120900	119600	115267	113534
1250000	130000	136500	135199	130000	127401

2.4.1d TABLE 4: Annual Income Range of Rs. 13 lakhs to Rs 15 lakhs

Income (INR)	Tax Liability under New Regime (INR)	Amount of Deductions (INR) At Break Even Point				
		216665	225000	233330	241670	250000
		Tax Liability under the Old Regime (INR)				
1300000	143000	143000	140400	137801	135199	132600
1350000	156000	158600	156000	153401	150799	148200
1400000	169000	174200	171600	169000	166399	163800
1450000	182000	189800	187200	184601	182000	179400
1500000	195000	205400	202800	200201	197599	195000

2.4.1e TABLE 5: Annual Income Range of Rs. 16 lakhs & Above

Income (INR)	Tax Liability under New Regime (INR)	Amount of Deductions (INR) At Break Even Point		
		250000	300000	350000
		Tax Liability under the Old Regime (INR)		
1600000	226200	226200	210600	195000
1700000	257400	257400	241800	226200
1800000	288600	288600	273000	257400
1900000	319800	319800	304200	288600
2000000	351000	351000	335400	319800

2.4.1f Comparative Sheet for Individuals/HUF having Business Income and are eligible for claiming additional depreciation u/s 32(1)(iia).

Cost of Machinery purchased: Rs. 10,00,000/-
Depreciation Rate u/s 32(1)(ii): 15%
Additional Depreciation Rate u/s 32(1)(iia): 20%
Date of Purchase: 01st April 2020

Tax Liability under the Old Regime:

(Amount in INR)

Income	Depreciation u/s 32(1)(ii)	Additional Depreciation u/s 32(1)(iia)	Net Income	Net Tax Liability
(A)	(B)	(C)	(A-B-C)	
500000	150000	200000	150000	0
600000	150000	200000	250000	0

700000	150000	200000	350000	0
750000	150000	200000	400000	0
800000	150000	200000	450000	0
900000	150000	200000	550000	23400
1000000	150000	200000	650000	44200
1100000	150000	200000	750000	65000
1200000	150000	200000	850000	85800

Tax Liability under the New Regime and the Net Tax Saving

(Amount in INR)

Income	Depreciation u/s 32(1)(ii)	Additional Depreciation u/s 32(1)(iia)	Net Income	Net Tax Liability	Net Savings in New Regime
(A)	(B)	(C)	(A-B-C)		
500000	150000	0	350000	0	0
600000	150000	0	450000	0	0

700000	150000	0	550000	18200	-18200
750000	150000	0	600000	23400	-23400
800000	150000	0	650000	28600	-28600
900000	150000	0	750000	39000	-15600
1000000	150000	0	850000	54600	-10400
1100000	150000	0	950000	70200	-5200
1200000	150000	0	1050000	88400	-2600

2.5 Time, Form & Manner of Exercise of Option for Availing the Benefit of Reduced Tax Rates u/s 115BAC

(i) the concessional rate shall not apply unless option is exercised by the individual or HUF in the form and manner as may be prescribed-

> a. where such individual or HUF has no business income, along with the return of income to be furnished under sub-section (1) of section 139 of the Act; and

> b. in any other case, on or before the due date specified under sub-section (1) of section 139 of the Act for furnishing the return of income for any previous year relevant to the assessment year commencing on or

after 1st April, 2021 and such option once exercised shall apply to subsequent assessment years.

2.6 Period of Exercising Option:

(i) An individual/HUF assessee, having no business or professional income, can exercise his option of choosing between the two tax regimes, every year, based on his entitlement of 'specified deductions'.

So, an individual/HUF assessee, having income under the heads 'Salary', 'House Property', 'Capital Gains' and 'Income from Other Sources', can opt for the new tax regime in one financial year, and can go back to the old tax regime in subsequent financial year, depending upon the circumstances and entitlement of 'specified deductions'.

(ii) An individual/HUF assessee, having business or professional income, can opt for the new tax regime of reduced taxes with no deductions, u/s 115BAC, only once and the option once exercised, for a previous year shall be valid for that previous year and all subsequent years.

(iii) The option of the new tax regime u/s 115BAC shall become invalid for a previous year or previous years, as the case may be, if the Individual or HUF fails to satisfy the conditions and other provisions as stipulated in section 115BAC of the Income Tax Act.

(iv) the option can be withdrawn only once where it was exercised by the individual or HUF having business income for a previous year other than the year in which it was exercised and thereafter, the individual or HUF shall never be eligible to exercise option under this section, except where such individual or HUF ceases to have any business income.

2.7 Concluding Remarks

In the preceding paragraphs, an honest and sincere attempt has been made to work out and analyse all the possible permutations and combinations of income levels of an individual and HUF assessee and the specified deductions, available to him, and a break-even point, between the old regime and the new regime of personal tax, in all the income levels, in terms of the availability of specified deductions, has been worked out.

Thus, these detailed computations will surely serve as a ready referencer for all the individual/HUF assessees and the tax professionals, to make informed and most appropriate choices of their tax structures in order to optimise their taxes.

Chapter 3

Decoding Vivad se Vishwaas Scheme 2020

3.1. The Hon'ble FM Smt. Nirmala Sitharaman in her Budget Speech, while presenting the Direct Tax Proposals, in the Finance Bill 2020, in the Parliament, on 1.2.2020, have asserted that,

"126. No Dispute but Trust Scheme – 'Vivad Se Vishwas' Scheme

- *Sir, in the past our Government has taken several measures to reduce tax litigations. In the last budget, Sabka Vishwas Scheme was brought in to reduce litigation in indirect taxes. It resulted in settling over 1,89,000 cases. Currently, there are 4,83,000 direct tax cases pending in various appellate forums i.e. Commissioner (Appeals), ITAT, High Court and Supreme Court. This year, I propose to bring a scheme similar to the indirect tax Sabka Vishwas for reducing litigations even in the direct taxes.*

- *Under the proposed 'Vivad Se Vishwas' scheme, a taxpayer would be required to pay only the amount of the disputed taxes and will get complete waiver of interest and penalty provided he pays by 31st March, 2020. Those who avail this scheme after 31st March, 2020 will have to pay some additional amount. The scheme will remain open till 30th June, 2020.*

- *Taxpayers in whose cases appeals are pending at any level can benefit from this scheme.*

- *I hope that taxpayers will make use of this opportunity to get relief from vexatious litigation process. "*

3.2 Promulgation of the *'Direct Tax Vivad se Vishwas Bill, 2020'*

Accordingly, the **Direct Tax Vivad se Vishwas Bill, 2020 ('the Scheme'),** has been introduced in the Lok Sabha on 05-02-2020, for dispute resolution related to direct taxes.

3.3 Objectives & Reasons:

The 'Statement of Objects and Reasons' of the *'Direct Tax Vivad se Vishwas Bill, 2020,* reads as under:

"Over the years, the pendency of appeals filed by taxpayers as well as Government has increased due to the fact that the number of appeals that are filed is much higher than the number of appeals that are disposed. As a result, a huge amount of disputed tax arrears is locked-up in these

appeals. As on the 30th November, 2019, the amount of disputed direct tax arrears is Rs. 9.32 lakh crores. Considering that the actual direct tax collection in the financial year 2018-19 was Rs.11.37 lakh crores, the disputed tax arrears constitute nearly one-year direct tax collection.

2. Tax disputes consume copious amount of time, energy and resources both on the part of the Government as well as taxpayers. Moreover, they also deprive the Government of the timely collection of revenue. Therefore, there is an urgent need to provide for resolution of pending tax disputes. This will not only benefit the Government by generating timely revenue but also the taxpayers who will be able to deploy the time, energy and resources saved by opting for such dispute resolution towards their business activities.

3. It is, therefore, proposed to introduce The Direct Tax Vivad se Vishwas Bill, 2020 for dispute resolution related to direct taxes…"

3.4 Key Features

3.4.1 Applicability/Eligibility (as amended by Union Cabinet):

a. All Appeals/Writs arising out of assessment/reassessment/TDS/TCS orders, filed by the assessee or income-tax authorities, pending as on 31st January, 2020, before:

- Commissioner of Income Tax (Appeals);
- Income Tax Appellate Tribunal;
- High Court of India;
- Supreme Court of India.

b. All Orders passed by AO/CIT(Appeals)/High Court on or before the specified date on 31.1.2020, and for which the statutory time for filing appeal/special leave petition, has not expired on 31.1.2020.

c. Cases pending before Dispute Resolution Panel (DRP) u/s 144C of Income Tax Act, on or before 31.1.2020.

d. Cases where DRP has issued directions on or before 31.1.2020, but no order has been passed.

e. Cases where assessee has filed Revision Application u/s 264 of Income Tax Act and such application are pending on 31.1.2020.

f. All Search Cases/Block Assessments u/s 153A/153C, where disputed demand is less than Rs. 5 crores.

3.4.2 Non-applicability/ Exclusions:

a. Where block assessment is made u/s 153A/153C pursuant to search and seizure proceedings u/s 132. However, the Union Cabinet on 12.2.2020, has expanded the scope of this scheme to cover the block assessment cases u/s 153A/153C also, where the disputed demand is below Rs. 5 crores.

Therefore, now, Search/Block Assessment Cases where disputed demand is more than Rs. 5 crores, only are excluded from the Scheme.

b. Where prosecution has been initiated under Income Tax Act or other Acts viz. the Prohibition of Benami Property Transactions Act, 1988, the Prevention of Money Laundering Act, the Prevention of Corruption Act, 1988 etc., before filing of declaration by the appellant;

c. Where there is undisclosed foreign income or asset;

d. Where case is initiated as per information exchange u/s 90/90A of the Income Tax Act, from other countries.

3.4.3 Tax Payable under the Scheme:

(I) Where the Appeals/Writs have been filed by the Assessees:

Nature of Tax Arrear	Amount payable up to 31-03-2020	Amount payable on or after 01-04-2020
Aggregate of disputed tax, interest chargeable and penalty on such disputed tax, in cases other than search/block assessments	100% of the amount of disputed tax	110% of the amount of disputed tax.
Aggregate of disputed tax, interest chargeable and penalty on such disputed tax, in cases of	125% of the amount of disputed tax	135% of the amount of disputed tax.

search/block assessments u/s 153A/153C, where disputed demand is less than Rs 5 crores		
Aggregate of disputed interest, penalty and disputed fee	25% of such disputed interest, penalty or fee	30% of such disputed interest, penalty or fee

(II) Where the Appeals/Writs have been filed by the Revenue Authorities:

Nature of Tax Arrear	Amount payable up to 31-03-2020	Amount payable on or after 01-04-2020
Aggregate of disputed tax, interest chargeable	50% of the amount of	55% of the amount of disputed tax.

and penalty on such disputed tax, in cases other than search/block assessments	disputed tax	
Aggregate of disputed tax, interest chargeable and penalty on such disputed tax, in cases of search/block assessments u/s 153A/153C, where disputed demand is less than Rs 5 crores	62.5% of the amount of disputed tax	67.5% of the amount of disputed tax.
Aggregate of disputed interest, penalty and disputed fee	12.5% of such disputed interest, penalty or fee	15% of such disputed interest, penalty or fee

a. 'Disputed Tax' in relation to an assessment year or financial year, means, the income-tax, including surcharge and cess, (hereinafter referred to as the amount of tax), payable by the appellant under Income Tax Act, as computed hereunder:

(i) in a case where any appeal, writ petition or special leave petition is pending before the appellate forum as on the specified date i.e. 31.1.2020, the amount of tax that is payable by the appellant, if such appeal, writ petition or special leave petition was to be decided against him;

(ii) in a case, where the order has been passed by the assessing officer on or before 31.1.2020, and the time for filing appeal against such order has not expired as on that date, the amount of tax payable by the appellant, in accordance with such order;

(iii) in a case, where an order in an appeal or in writ petition has been passed by the appellate forum on or before 31.1.2020, and the time for filing appeal or special leave petition against such order has not expired as on that date, the amount of tax payable by the appellant, after giving effect to the order so passed;

(iv) in a case, where objection filed by the appellant is pending before the Dispute Resolution Panel u/s 144C of Income Tax Act as on 31.1.2020, the amount of tax payable by the appellant, if the Dispute Resolution Panel was to confirm the variation proposed in the draft order;

(v) in a case, where Dispute Resolution Panel has issued any direction u/s 144C(5) of Income Tax Act, and the assessing officer has not passed the order u/s 144C(13) on or before 31.1.2020, the amount of tax payable by the appellant as per the assessment order to be passed by the assessing officer u/s 144C(13) of Income Tax Act;

(vi) in a case where an application for revision u/s 264 of Income Tax Act is pending as on 31.1.2020, the amount of tax payable by the appellant, if such application for revision was not to be accepted.

(vii) in a case, where the assessing officer has reduced the returned loss by making addition of income/ disallowance of expenditure, the appellant shall have an option

- to either pay the tax on amount by which the loss has been reduced and carry forward the entire loss without any reduction; or

- to carry forward the reduced loss (after adjusting such addition/disallowance), without making any payment of tax.

(viii) in a case, where CIT(Appeals) has issued a notice of enhancement u/s 251 of Income Tax Act, on or before 31.1.2020, the disputed tax shall be increased by the amount of tax pertaining to issues for which notice of enhancement has been issued.

(ix) in a case, where the appellant has obtained a favourable decision/order from ITAT/High Court, on an issue, the amount of tax payable would be 50% of the disputed tax on such issue.

(x) tax determined under the section 200A or section 201 or subsection (6A) of section 206C or section 206CB of the Income-tax Act, 1961, i.e. TDS or TCS, in respect of which appeal has been filed by the appellant.

b. **'Disputed interest'** means any interest determined under the provisions of the Act (not being an interest charged or chargeable on disputed tax) against which appeal has been filed and pending before the appellate forum.

c. **'Disputed penalty'** means any penalty determined under the provisions of the Act (not being a penalty levied or leviable on disputed income or disputed tax) against which appeal has been filed and pending before the appellate forum.

d. **'Disputed fee'** means any fee which is determined as per the provisions of the Act against which appeal has been filed and pending before the appellate forum.

(iv) 'Last date' may be notified later although announced as 30th June, 2020 in the Budget Speech

3.4.4 Procedure:

a. The appellant shall file a declaration to the designated authority in the notified form electronically.

Section 2(1)(*a*) of the 'The Direct Tax Vivad se Vishwaas Bill 2020, defines the term 'appellant' as under:

"appellant" means the person or the income-tax authority or both who has filed appeal before the appellate forum and such appeal is pending on the specified date."

Section 2(1)(d) of the 'The Direct Tax Vivad se Vishwaas Bill 2020, defines the term 'declaration' as under:

"declaration" means the declaration filed under section 4."

Section 4(1) of the 'The Direct Tax Vivad se Vishwaas Bill 2020, provides as under:

"4. (1) The declaration referred to in section 3 shall be filed by the declarant before the designated authority in such form and verified in such manner as may be prescribed."

The form and the manner of verification is yet to be prescribed by the Law Makers.

c. In case where the taxpayer makes any false statement or violates any condition, the declaration filed by him will be deemed to have never been made and the pending dispute will get revived.

d. The designated authority, within 15 days of the receipt of such declaration, shall determine the amount payable by the appellant and may grant a certificate to the appellant stating the particulars of tax arrears and the amount payable.

Section 2(*e*) of the 'The Direct Tax Vivad se Vishwaas Bill 2020, defines the term 'designated authority as under:

"designated authority" means an officer not below the rank of a Commissioner of Income-tax notified by the Principal Chief Commissioner for the purposes of this Act."

e. Upon the filing of the declaration, where the appeal in respect of the disputed income or disputed interest or disputed penalty or disputed fee and tax arrears, is pending before the CIT(A) or ITAT, the same shall be deemed to have been withdrawn, from the date on which certificate as per point no. d, above, is issued by the designated authority.

c. Where the appeal is pending before the High Court (in a writ or appeal) or in Supreme Court, the appellant has to withdraw the said appeal/ writ with the leave of the court and furnish the proof along with the declaration to be filed with designated authority.

d. Where, the appellant is in any arbitration under any law or tax treaties, he has to withdraw it and furnish the proof along with the declaration.

e. The appellant is also required to furnish an undertaking waiving his right, that may be available to him under any law or any tax treaty with respect to the tax arrears.

f. Within 15 days of the receipt of the certificate, the appellant shall pay the amount as stated in the certificate and intimate the same to the designated authority.

g. The designated authority shall pass the order and all disputed tax, interest, penalty and fees shall be deemed to be withdrawn from the date of the certificate.

h. The order passed by the designated authority shall be final, and as a result, the Appellate Authority or arbitrators or mediator shall be barred from proceeding with the appeal.

i. Every order passed by the designated authority, as per point g, above, determining the amount payable under this Act, shall be conclusive as to the matters stated therein and no matter covered by such order shall be reopened in any other proceeding under the Income-tax Act or under any other law for the time being in force or under any agreement, whether for protection of investment or otherwise, entered into by India with any other country or territory outside India.

j. The designated authority shall not institute any proceeding in respect of an offence, or impose or levy any penalty, or charge any interest under the Income-tax Act in respect of tax arrears.

k. Any amount paid in pursuance of a declaration made under section 4 shall not be refundable under any circumstances.

3.5 Some Provisions in the Bill, requiring more Clarity and/or Relaxations, from the Law Makers:

a. Further Relaxation in the Amount of Tax to be paid if Disputed Tax falls under section 115BBE.

The nomenclature of this dispute resolution scheme i.e. 'Vivad se Vishwaas Scheme' suggests the 'trust-centric' philosophy and intent of the Law Makers behind bringing out this Tax Amnesty Scheme.

It has been asserted that this dispute resolution scheme would benefit primarily in the disputes concerning cash deposit cases in demonetisation period and penny stock cases.

In all such cases, the provisions of section 115BBE have been pressed into service by the Revenue Authorities and an effective tax rate of almost 78% (Basic Rate u/s 115BBE @ 60% plus surcharge @ 25%), has been levied on the additions.

Therefore, in all such cases, even the 'disputed tax' @ 78%, is very high and may not be persuasive enough to motivate the assessee to opt for this scheme.

Therefore, in order to bring fruitful results in such cases, under this scheme, the amount of 'disputed tax' to be paid by the appellant, should be reduced to the maximum marginal rate of tax of approximately 33.66% and not at the high rate of 78%. If at all, some differentiation is to be made between normal cases and such cases, then a higher rate of say 40% may be prescribed, so as to ensure fruitful tax realisation, in such cases, under the scheme.

b. Choice of going for appeal for partial additions is not available to the appellant:

Amount payable being the disputed tax is so defined that the said tax is to be computed for the whole of the additions in respect of which appeal is filed.

In other words, if there are more than one issue involved in the appeal, the appellant would be mandatorily required to file his declaration u/s 4 for all the issues.

Hence, one cannot go ahead to resolve litigation for certain issues and continue the litigation for other issues and as such the choice of going for appeal for partial additions is not available, to the appellant, which should be given, to impart greater flexibility to the appellant.

c. Timeline for carrying out pending rectification u/s 154 of the Income Tax Act, should be given:

There may be cases where rectification as regard to non- granting of proper set-off of brought forward losses on account of computation error, etc. are pending at the end of the jurisdictional Assessing Officer/ CPC which have an impact in determining the correct tax on Total Income. In absence of carrying out such rectification in a timely manner, the amount payable for the disputed tax cannot be determined correctly u/s. 5(1).

d. No Option to challenge the arithmetical correctness of amount payable:

As per the section 5(1) of the Bill, the designated authority is required to determine the amount payable by the declarant and grant a certificate to the declarant containing particulars of the tax arrears and the amount payable after such determination, in such form as may be prescribed.

In the current provisions of the Act, after such determination of amount payable by the designated authority, there is no option on the part of the declarant to either move a rectification application or challenge its arithmetical correctness before any higher authority.

e. Authentic and Proper Adjustments of Amount of Taxes already paid earlier:

The amount of tax to be paid under the scheme u/s 5(2) of the Bill includes the payment towards disputed taxes which have already been paid earlier. It has been provided that, the appellant shall be entitled for refund, if the amount already paid by the appellant before filing declaration u/s 4, exceeds the amount of tax payable under this scheme.

However, still for more certainty, the declaration form so to be prescribed should clearly provide for relevant columns/fields for ensuring correct and proper disclosures/adjustments and resultant refunds in cases where excess amount is already paid earlier.

f. Requirement of Extension of this Scheme to Block Assessment Cases u/s 153A/153C, where the disputed tax demand is more than Rs. 5 crores.

The Scheme covers only assessment and reassessment cases and the block assessment cases u/s 153A/153C, where the disputed tax demand is less than Rs. 5 crores.

It needs to be appreciated that majority of the appeals/disputes arise on account of block assessments involving recovery of more than Rs. 5

crores, and as such substantial 'vivad' arises on account of such block assessments only.

Therefore, keeping such block assessments, outside the purview of this scheme, may not bring the desired fruits and tax realisation under the scheme. So, the scheme needs to be extended to block assessments u/s 153A/153C involving recovery of more than Rs. 5 crores also, to justify the name of this Scheme, 'Vivad se Vishwaas Scheme'.

Chapter 4

Restrictions on Powers of ITAT to Grant Stay of Demand

4.1 Stipulation of Compulsory Deposition of atleast 20% of outstanding income tax demand, by the assessee, so as to enable the ITAT to Grant Stay of Demand.

Another significant amendment which has been proposed in the Finance Bill 2020, although not referred to in the Budget Speech is the amendment in the proviso to section 254(2A) of the Act to provide that ITAT may grant stay under the first proviso subject to the condition that the assessee deposits not less than twenty per cent of the amount of tax, interest, fee, penalty, or any other sum payable under the provisions of this Act, or furnish security of equal amount in respect thereof.

The existing provisions of the first proviso to sub-section (2A) of section 254 of the Act, *inter-alia*, provides that the ITAT may, after considering the merits of the application made by the assessee pass an order of stay for a maximum period of 180 days in any proceedings against the order of the Commissioner of Income-tax (Appeal). Second proviso to the said sub-section prescribes that where the appeal is not so disposed of, the ITAT on being satisfied that the delay is not attributable to the assessee, extend the stay for a further period subject to the restriction that the aggregate of the periods originally allowed and the period so extended shall not, in any case, exceed 365 days and the Appellate Tribunal shall dispose of the appeal within the period or periods of stay so extended or allowed. The third proviso of the said sub-section also provides that if such appeal is not so disposed of within the period allowed under the first proviso or the period or periods extended or allowed under the second proviso, which shall not, in any case, exceed 365 days, the order of stay shall stand vacated after the expiry of such period or periods, even if the delay in disposing of the appeal is not attributable to the assessee.

It has been proposed in the Finance Bill 2020, to provide that ITAT may grant stay under the first proviso subject to the condition that the assessee deposits not less than twenty per cent of the amount of tax, interest, fee, penalty, or any other sum payable under the provisions of this Act, or furnish security of equal amount in respect thereof.

It has also been proposed to substitute second proviso to provide that no extension of stay shall be granted by ITAT, where such appeal is not so disposed of within the said period of stay as specified in the order of stay. However, on an application made by the assessee, a further stay can be granted, if the delay in not disposing of the appeal is not attributable to the assessee and the assessee has deposited not less than twenty per cent of the amount of tax, interest, fee, penalty, or any other sum payable under the provisions of this Act, or furnish security of equal amount in respect thereof. The total stay granted by ITAT cannot exceed 365 days.

This amendment will take effect from 1st April, 2020, and is applicable from AY 2021-22, onwards.

It is pertinent to mention here that in existing provisions of section 254(2A), the ITAT was having full power to grant stay of income tax demand, even an absolute stay of demand, in deserving cases, if it finds it appropriate as per the provisions of Law. However, now this proposed amendment has made this power of ITAT to grant stay of demand, conditional on the deposition of atleast 20% of the outstanding demand by the assessee.

4.2 Effect of Stipulation of Compulsory Deposition of 20% Demand on High Pitched Assessments

The above dictum of deposition of atleast 20% of outstanding income tax demand, as a mandatory pre-condition for obtaining stay of demand from ITAT, even in the cases of high-pitched assessments, wherein assessed income is twice or more than the returned income, needs to be analysed and seen from the legal perspective also.

In the cases of high-pitched assessments, the legal position of grant of an absolute stay of demand, was well-settled, as per numerous binding legal precedents.

However, this proposed amendment, will force the assessee to deposit atleast 20% of the outstanding demand, for making his/her application for stay of demand being admitted and entertained by the ITAT, in all the cases including high-pitched assessments.

It will be in the fitness of things to consider the relevant CBDT Circulars and the related judicial pronouncements having a direct bearing on the issue of stay of grant in high pitched assessment cases.

The First CBDT Instruction addressing the issue of Grant of Stay of Demand in High Pitched Assessments was CBDT Instruction No. 95 dated 21.8.1969. It categorically provided that,

"Where the income determined on assessment was substantially higher than the returned income, say twice the latter amount or more, the collection of the tax in dispute should be held in abeyance till the decision on the appeal provided there were no lapses on the part of the assesses."

Therefore, the said CBDT Instruction, very clearly provided that in case of high- pitched assessments, the tax recovery proceedings should be kept in abeyance and the stay of grant should be provided by the assessing authorities to the assessees, till the disposal of appeal by the appellate authority.

Then CBDT had come up with another Instruction No. 1914 dated 2.12.1993, on Stay of Demand, and the Revenue Authorities contended that all previous instructions stood superseded by the said instruction, which included the supersession of the earlier CBDT Instruction No. 95 dated 21.8.1969, also.

This matter was the subject matter of consideration in the judgment of the Hon'ble Delhi High Court in the case of *"Taneja Developers and Infrastracture*

Ltd., Vs. Assistant Commissioner of Income Tax, Delhi and Ors in W.P.(C).No.6956 of 2009, (2009) 222 CTR (Del) 521 dated 24.02.2009, wherin the Hon'ble Delhi High Court, relying upon its earlier judgment in the case of *"Valvoline Cummins Ltd. v. CIT and Ors. (2008) 217 CTR (Del) 292,* had categorically held as under,

"9.Having considered the arguments advanced by the learned counsel for the parties, we are of the view that although Instruction No.1914 of 1993 specifically states that it is in supersession of all earlier instructions, the position obtaining after the decision of this Court in Valvoline Cummins Ltd., (Supra) is not altered at all. This is so because paragraph No.2(A) which speaks of responsibility specifically indicates that it shall be the responsibility of the Assessing Officer and the TRO to collect every demand that has been raised except the following', which includes: (d) demand stayed in accordance with the paras B and C below. Para B relates to stay petitions. As extracted above, Sub-clause (iii) of para B clearly indicates that a higher/superior authority could interfere with the decision of the Assessing Officer/TRO only in exceptional circumstances. The exceptional circumstances have been indicated as – "where the assessment order appears to be unreasonably high pitched or where genuine hardship is likely to be

caused to the assessee.... The very question as to what would constitute the assessment order as being reasonably high pitched in consideration under the said Instruction No.96 and, there, it has been noted by way of illustration that assessment at twice the amount of the returned income would amount to being substantially higher or high pitched. In the case before this Court in Valvoline Cummins Ltd., (supra) that assessee's income was about eight (8) times the returned income. This Court was of the view that was high pitched. In the present case, the assessed income is approximately 74 times the returned income and obviously, this would fall within the expression unreasonably high pitched. (Emphasis supplied)...

A reading of the above dictum would show that if assessment order is unreasonably high pitched or genuine hardship is likely to be caused to the assessee, then the assessee is entitled to be treated as not being in default in respect of the amount in dispute in the appeal."

Then CBDT had again come up with CBDT Office Memorandum dated 29.2.2016, which provides that a Stay of Demand may be granted to the assessee on deposition of 15% (further increased to 20% by CBDT office memorandum dated 31.7.2017), of the total outstanding income tax demand, if the assessee's appeal is pending before the

CIT(Appeals). The assessing authorities, by virtue of the said CBDT Office Memorandums, as a matter of their inherent right, by default, are pressurizing for deposition of atleast 20% of the total income tax demand, even in cases of high- pitched assessments.

However, again the third pillar of democracy, i.e. the Judiciary, has come to the rescue of the assessees.

In a recent judgement of the Hon'ble Karnataka High Court, in the case of *M/s Flipkart India Pvt Ltd vs ACIT, Circle 3(1)(1), vide Writ Petition Nos. 1339-1342/2017 (T-IT), 23.2.2017,* the Hon'ble High Court has categorically held as follows:

Para 16 "*.....It is true that Instruction No.4 (B)(b) of the Circular dated 29.2.2016, gives two instances where less than 15% can be asked to be deposited. However, it is equally true that the factors, which were directed to be kept in mind both by the Assessing Officer, and by the higher superior authority, contained in Instruction No.2-B(iii) of Circular No.1914, still continue to exist. For, as noted above, the said part of Circular No.1914 has been left untouched by the Circular dated 29.2.2016. Therefore, while dealing with an application filed by an assessee, both the Assessing Officer, and the Prl. CIT, are required to see if the assessee's case would fall under Instruction No.2-B(iii) of Circular No.1914, or not? Both the Assessing Officer, and the*

Prl. CIT, are required to examine whether the assessment is "unreasonably high pitched", or whether the demand for depositing 15% of the disputed demand amount "would lead to a genuine hardship being caused to the assessee" or not?

The principal ratios emerging from the aforesaid High Court judgments clearly provide that in the cases of high-pitched assessments, the stipulation of blanket deposition of atleast 20% of the income tax demand, is not applicable and stay of demand ought to be granted to the assessees, by the assessing authorities.

The Law Makers should appreciate that the compulsory deposition of atleast 20% of the exorbitant and arbitrary income-tax demand in high pitched assessment cases, by the assessees, so as to enable them to file their applications for stay of demand, before the ITAT, would result in a lot of financial and other hardships to the assessees and would also make the right of their appeal totally meaningless and nugatory.

Therefore, it needs to be seen as to whether this proposed amendment will muster the test of well-settled and established principles of Law, at appropriate appellate forums.

Chapter 5

Penalty for False Entry/False Invoice: Section 271AAD

5.1 Insertion of New Section 271AAD

The Finance Bill 2020 has proposed to insert a new section 271AAD in the Income Tax Act, to provide for a levy of penalty on persons in the cases of false entries or omission of entries, in the books being maintained by such persons, with a view to evade tax.

It has been proposed in the Finance Bill 2020, that if it is found during any proceeding under the Act that in the books of accounts maintained by any person, there is a:

(i) false entry or;

(ii) any entry relevant for computation of total income of such person has been omitted to evade tax liability,

then a penalty u/s 271AAD shall be levied, on such person.

The penalty payable by such person shall be equal to the aggregate amount of false entries or omitted entry.

It has also been proposed to provide that any other person, who causes in any manner a person to make or cause to make a false entry or omits or causes to omit any entry, shall also pay by way of penalty a sum which is equal to the aggregate amounts of such false entries or omitted entry.

The connotation **'false entries'**, include use or intention to use –

(a) forged or falsified documents such as a false invoice or, in general, a false piece of documentary evidence; or

(b) invoice in respect of supply or receipt of goods or services or both issued by the person or any other person without actual supply or receipt of such goods or services or both; or

(c) invoice in respect of supply or receipt of goods or services or both to or from a person who do not exist. This amendment will take effect from 1st April, 2020.

This amendment will take effect from 1st April, 2020 and as such shall be applicable w.e.f. AY 2021 onwards

5.2 Purpose & Objective:

The Memorandum to the Finance Bill 2020, has explained the rationale and the need to insert the above provision in the Act, as under:

"In the recent past after the launch of Goods & Services Tax (GST), several cases of fraudulent input tax credit (ITC) claim have been caught by the GST authorities. In these cases, fake invoices are obtained by suppliers registered under GST to fraudulently claim ITC and reduce their GST liability. These invoices are found to be issued by racketeers who do not actually carry on any business or profession. They only issue invoices without actually supplying any goods or services. The GST shown to have been charged on such invoices is neither paid nor is intended to be paid. Such fraudulent arrangements deserve to be dealt with harsher provisions under the Act."

5.3 Effect of the newly inserted Section 271AAD on Income Tax Jurisprudence concerning Accommodation/Bogus Entries

Though the primary reason for insertion of this new section 271AAD in the Income Tax Act, has been to curb the malpractice of availment of bogus input tax credit (ITC) under the GST Law, however, the same, will definitely cause a lot of ripples and repercussions, in the income tax jurisprudence, concerning accommodation/bogus entries.

As has already been explained above that under the new section 271AAD, a penalty of 100% of the amount of false/bogus entries/bogus purchase invoices, has been proposed in the Finance Bill 2020, on the person, in whose books of accounts, such entries are being found and also on any other person who causes in any manner a person to make or cause to make a false entry or omits or causes to omit any entry.

It is pertinent to mention here, that in several judgements of different High Courts and even Supreme Court, it has been held that even in the cases of bogus purchase entries, the entire bogus purchase entries can't be disallowed, and only an appropriate NP rate may be added, if the purchases are correlated with the corresponding sales/closing stock.

It is a well settled and established principle of Law that the assessing officer cannot blow both hot and cold simultaneously by accepting the sales and closing stock and rejecting the corresponding purchases. Reliance in this regard is placed upon a very recent decision of the jurisdictional Hon'ble

Delhi ITAT in the case of "Agson Global Pvt Ltd vs. ACIT in ITA No. 3741-3746 and 5264-5269/Del/2019 dated 31.10.2019. Thus, as in the present case the ld. AO has duly accepted the sales and closing stock of the assessee company as per its audited books of accounts, then he is not lawfully entitled to discredit and reject the corresponding purchases being undertaken by the assessee company to generate the said sales and closing stocks.

Reliance in this regard is placed upon the binding judgements of:

(i) **PCIT vs. Tejua Rohit Kumar Kapadia (2018) 94 taxmann.com 325 (SC);**

(ii) **CIT vs. Odeon Builders Pvt Ltd in Appeal Nos. 9604-9605 of 2018 dated 21.8.2019 (SC);**

(iii) **CIT vs. Bholanath Poly Fab (P) Ltd 355 ITR 290;**

(iv) **CIT vs. Simit P.Seth 356 ITR 451;**

(v) **CIT vs. Satyanarayan P. Rathi 351 ITR 150**

Therefore, this proposed amendment will definitely have some major repercussions, as far as the settled and established position of Law concerning additions in relation to false/accommodation/bogus entries, is concerned.

It also needs to be seen and ensured that the double taxation u/s 69A/69B and under this new section 271AAD, is not being made by the assessing authorities, and 'Standard Operating Procedures' (SOPs), are being laid out by the Legislature, so as to eliminate the element of subjectivity and uncertainty in treating the entries in the books of accounts as false, so as to trigger the applicability of this new section 271AAD.

Chapter 6

Charitable Trusts, Educational Institutes, Universities, Schools, Hospitals and Other such Institutions

6.1 Off late, the Charitable Trusts and Organisations have been in the focus and radar of income tax authorities' close scrutiny, and the Government is continuously tightening the laws to bring more transparency in the working of such organisations.

The Finance Bill 2020 has also not been so *'Charitable'* when it came to incorporating provisions and making amendments in the Legislature concerning Charitable Trusts and Institutions.

6.2 Major Amendments concerning Charitable Trusts/ Educational Institutions & Hospitals in Finance Bill 2020

Some of the prominent and significant amendments concerning charitable trusts and similar organisations, which have been proposed in the Finance Bill 2020, are being discussed and analysed as under:

i) Registration of Charitable Trusts u/s 12A/80G, Educational Institutions & Hospitals u/s 10(23C)/80G and similar organisations u/s 35 of the Act, to be valid for a period of 5 years only and not for an indefinite period.

The Finance Bill 2020 has proposed that the registration of charitable trusts u/s 12A/12AA and 80G, educational institutions & hospitals u/s 10(23C) and similar organisations u/s 35 of the Act, is to remain valid for a period of 5 years only and not for an indefinite period, as has been currently provided in the Act.

a. Existing Registered Entities:

In order to ensure that the conditions of registration are being adhered to, all the existing charitable trusts and organisations registered u/s 12A/12AA and all the educational institutions and hospitals registered u/s 10(23C) of the Act, have to compulsorily apply afresh for their registration under the respective sections, within a period of three months from June 1, 2020.

It is expected and desirable that in granting the approval for re-registration u/s 12A/10(23CA)/35/80G of the Act, the competent Income Tax Authority i.e. the Principal Commissioner of Income tax or the Commissioner of

Income tax, shall not conduct detailed enquiries, and such re-registrations shall be done, immediately after receiving the applications from the respective entities. However, with the implementation of these provisions, and with the passage of time, more clarity will emerge.

Any failure, lapse or omission on the part of the existing registered entities u/s 12A/10(23C)/80G/35, to apply for renewal of their registration before the competent tax authorities within the stipulated time period of 1st June 2020 till 31st August 2020, would result in losing of their registration status under the respective sections.

Therefore, all the existing registered entities u/s 12A/10(23C)/80G/35, have to compulsorily comply with the proposed stipulation of applying for the renewal of their registration, uptill 31.8.2020, so as to continue with their tax-exempt registered status.

b. New Entities

All new charitable trusts and organisations making applications for their registration u/s 12AA/80G and educational institutions & hospitals u/s 10(23C)/80G, shall be provisionally approved or registered for three years on the basis of application without detailed enquiry even in the cases where activities of the entity are yet to begin and then the said entities have to apply again for approval or registration which, if granted, shall be valid for a period of five years, from the date of such provisional registration. The application of registration subsequent to provisional registration should be made at least six months prior to expiry of provisional registration or within six months of start of activities, whichever is earlier.

(ii) Filing of statement of donation by donee to cross-check claim of donation by donor:

It has been proposed in the Finance Bill 2020 that deduction u/s 80G/ 80GGA to a donor shall be allowed only if a statement is furnished by the donee, who shall be required to furnish a statement in respect of donations received and in the event of failure to do so, fee and penalty shall be levied.

(iii) Existing Registrations u/s 12A of Educational Institutions & Hospitals, would be made inoperative, from the date of their registration u/s 10(23C) of the Act

As per the existing provisions in the Legislature, there is no bar or restriction for an educational institution or a hospital to obtain registration u/s 10(23C) as well as u/s 12AA of the Act.

So, in case of any lapse in compliance of the registration conditions of any one of these sections viz. 12A or 10(23C), these entities could still enjoy the benefits of exemption under the second section.

However, the Finance Bill has proposed to do away with this flexible regime and has proposed that registration under section 12AA would become inoperative in case of an entity exempt under clause (23C) of section 10. If the entity wishes to make it operative in the future, it will have to file an application and then it would not be entitled for deduction u/s 10(23C), from the date on which the registration u/s 12AA, becomes operative.

(iv) Restrictions on Cash Donations u/s 80GGA to Rs. 2000/- only

It has been proposed in the Finance Bill 2020, that similar to section 80G of the Act, deduction of cash donation u/s 80GGA shall be restricted to Rs. 2,000/- only.

These amendments will take effect from 1st June, 2020.

"Charity begins at home but should not end there." *–Francis Bacon*

6.3 Business Trusts

"Benevolence today has become altogether too huge an undertaking to be conducted otherwise than on business lines." –Julius Rosenwald

Modification of the definition of "business trust"

The definition of "business trust" has been provided in clause (13A) of section 2 of the Act, to mean a trust registered as an Infrastructure Investment Trust (InvIT) or a Real Estate Investment Trust (REIT) under the relevant regulations made under the Securities and Exchange Board of India (SEBI) Act, 1992 and the units of which are required to be listed on a recognised stock exchange in accordance with the relevant regulations.

Section 115UA of the Act provides for a taxation regime applicable to business trusts. Under the said regime, the total income of the trust, excluding capital gains income is charged at the maximum marginal rate. Further, the income by way of interest and rent, received by the business trust from a Special Purpose Vehicle (SPV) is accorded pass through treatment i.e. there is no taxation of such interest or rental income in the hands of the trust and no withholding tax at the level of SPV. The business trusts are also required to furnish return of income and adhere to other reporting requirements.

Representations have been received stating that private unlisted InvITs should be given the same status as public listed InvITs with regards to tax treatments provided under the Act.

Securities and Exchange Board of India (Infrastructure Investment Trusts) (Amendment) (Regulations), 2019 vide notification No.SEBI/LAD-NRO/GN/2019/10 has, *inter-alia*, done away with the mandatory listing requirement for InvITs.

In light of this, the definition of business trusts under the Act is required to be aligned with the amended SEBI Regulations.

Therefore, it has been proposed in the Finance Bill to amend clause (13A) of section 2 of the Act to modify the definition of "business trust" so as to do away with the requirement of the units of business trust to be listed on a recognised stock exchange.

This amendment will take effect from 1st April, 2021 and will, accordingly, apply in relation to the AY 2021-22 and subsequent assessment years.

Chapter 7

Faceless e-Appeals & e-Penalty: One More Step towards Digital Transformation of Indian Tax Administration

7.1 Insertion of Legislative Provisions in Finance Bill 2020 for 'Faceless e-Appeals & e-Penalty'

Continuing with its legacy of Digital Transformation of Indian Tax Administration, the Finance Bill 2020, presented by the Hon'ble FM Smt. Nirmala Sitharaman in the Parliament on 1.2.2020, has inserted the enabling provisions in the Income Tax Act, so as to facilitate the incorporation of the 'new scheme of faceless e-appeals and e-penalty', to be notified in near future, similar to the already notified scheme of faceless e-assessments 2019.

It is pertinent to mention here that in order to impart greater efficiency, transparency and accountability to the assessment process under the Act, the Finance Act 2018, has already incorporated the enabling provisions for enacting the 'New Scheme of Faceless e-Assessments' in the Legislature, by way of inserting three new subsections viz. (3A), (3B) and (3C) in section 143 of the Income Tax Act, 1961.

Accordingly, in exercise of the powers conferred by sub-section (3A) of section 143 of the Income-tax Act, 1961, the Central Government has incorporated a new scheme of assessment known as "E-Assessment Scheme 2019" by way of Official Gazetted Notifications No. SO 3264 or 61/2019 dated 12.9.2019. In the first phase, the Income-tax department has selected 58,322 cases for scrutiny under the 'New Scheme of E-assessment-2019', for the AY 2018-19, which are getting time barred on 30.9.2020.

7.2 Faceless e-Appeal

With the advent of the e-assessment scheme, most of the functions/ processes under the Act, including of filing of return, processing of returns, issuance of refunds or demand notices and assessment, which used to require person-to-person contact between the taxpayer and the Income-tax Department, are now in the electronic mode. This is a result of efforts by the Department to harness the power of technology in reforming the system. All these processes are now not only faceless but also very taxpayer-friendly. Now a taxpayer can manage to comply with most of his obligations under the Act without any requirement for physical attendance in the offices of the Department.

The filing of appeals before Commissioner (Appeals) has already been enabled in an electronic mode. However, the first appeal process under the Commissioner (Appeals), which is one of the major functions/ processes that is not yet in full electronic mode. A taxpayer can file appeal through his registered account on the e-filing portal. However, the process that follows after filing of appeal is neither electronic nor faceless. In order to ensure that the reforms initiated by the Department to eliminate human interface from the system reach the next level, it is imperative that an e-appeal scheme be launched on the lines of e-assessment scheme.

Accordingly, it is proposed to insert sub-section (6A) in section 250 of the Act to provide for the following: –

- Empowering Central Government to notify an e-appeal scheme for disposal of appeal so as to impart greater efficiency, transparency and accountability.

- Eliminating the interface between the Commissioner (Appeals) and the appellant in the course of appellate proceedings to the extent technologically feasible.

- Optimizing utilization of the resources through economies of scale and functional specialisation.

- Introducing an appellate system with dynamic jurisdiction in which appeal shall be disposed of by one or more Commissioner (Appeals).

It is also proposed to empower the Central Government, for the purpose of giving effect to the scheme made under the proposed sub-section, by notification in the Official Gazette, to direct that any of the provisions of this Act relating to jurisdiction and procedure of disposal of appeal shall not apply or shall apply with such exceptions, modifications and adaptations as may be specified in the notification. Such directions are to be issued on or before 31st March 2022. It is proposed that every notification issued shall be required to be laid before each House of Parliament.

This amendment will take effect from 1st April, 2020.

7.3 Faceless e-Penalty

Section 274 of the Act provides for the procedure for imposing penalty under Chapter XXI of the Act. In response to a showcause notice issued by the Assessing Officer (AO), assessee or his authorised representative is still required to visit the office of the Assessing Officer. With the advent of the E-Assessment Scheme-2019 and in order to ensure that the reforms initiated by the Department to eliminate human interface from the system reaches the next level, it is imperative that an e-penalty scheme be launched on the lines of E-assessment Scheme-2019.

Therefore, it has been proposed in the Finance Bill 2020 to insert a new sub-section (2A) in the said section so as to provide that the Central Government may notify an e-scheme for the purposes of imposing penalty so as to impart greater efficiency, transparency and accountability by —

(a) eliminating the interface between the Assessing Officer and the assessee in the course of proceedings to the extent technologically feasible;

(b) optimising utilisation of the resources through economies of scale and functional specialisation;

(c) introducing a mechanism for imposing of penalty with dynamic jurisdiction in which penalty shall be imposed by one or more income-tax authorities.

It has also been proposed to empower the Central Government, for the purpose of giving effect to the scheme made under the proposed sub-section, for issuing notification in the Official Gazette, to direct that any of the provisions of this Act relating to jurisdiction and procedure of imposing penalty shall not apply or shall apply with such exceptions, modifications and adaptations as may be specified in the notification. Such directions are to be issued on or before 31st March, 2022. It is proposed that every notification issued shall be required to be laid before each House of Parliament.

This amendment will take effect from 1st April, 2020.

7.4 Enlarging the Scope of Faceless e-Assessment Scheme 2019 to include Ex-parte Best Judgements Assessments u/s 144 of the Act

Section 143 of the Act provides the manner for processing and assessment of return of income (ITR) where a return has been made under section 139, or in response to a notice under sub-section (1) of section 142 of the Act.

Sub-section (3A) of section 143 provides that the Central Government may make a scheme, by notification in the Official Gazette, for the purposes of making assessment of total income or loss of the assessee under sub-section (3) of section 143 so as to impart greater efficiency, transparency and accountability by certain means specified therein. Accordingly, E-assessment Scheme, 2019 was notified under sub-section (3A) of Section 143 of the Act.

It has been proposed to amend sub-section (3A) of section 143 of the Act to-

(i)   expand the scope so as to include the reference of section 144 of the Act relating to best judgement assessment in the said sub-section;

(ii)   provide that Central Government may issue any direction under sub-section (3B) of the said section up to 31st March, 2022.

This amendment will take effect from 1st April, 2020.

7.5 Way Forward

In order to make these path-breaking, radical and revolutionary initiatives of the 'faceless' and 'jurisdiction-less' 'e-assessments, e-appeals and e-penalty', effective and taxpayer friendly, it is essential and crucial to issue appropriate clarifications with regard to the exact modus operandi of the functionality of such schemes and to take suitable measures and steps to overcome the initial bottlenecks and hurdles by way of ensuring the commensurate and supporting IT infrastructure to enable seamless and smooth data transfer, incorporating standardization in the conduct of assessments, appeals and penalty proceedings by Income Tax authorities, by implementing Standard Operating Procedures (SOPs) to do away with the subjective-ness and arbitrariness, and fixing proper and effective accountability in cases of high pitched assessments.

So, all the stakeholders involved i.e. the taxpayers, the tax professionals, the assessing authorities, the regulatory body CBDT, the Finance Ministry and the Government should embrace these radical, revolutionary and path-breaking reforms of *'Faceless e-Assessments, e-Appeals and e-Penalty'* in good and positive spirits and should work collectively and cohesively to make this initiative a grand success.

It is only then perhaps that these reforms and initiatives aimed at digital transformation of Indian Tax Administration, will really live up to their true potential, and taxpayers as well as the tax administration authorities will reap the benefits that these are supposed to provide.

Useful Reference: For More Details and Complete Understanding of the nitty-gritties and nuances of the New Scheme of Faceless e-Assessments 2019, the recently published **Book titled "Guide to e-Assessment with Real-time Case Studies & Suggestive e-Submissions"**, authored by the author of this Book and published by Taxmann Publications, may be referred, which is a ready referencer and user manual to help and assist the assessees and the assessing authorities in their 'e-Assessment pursuits'.

"No Body Can Stop an Idea Whose Time Has Come!!" - Victor Hugo

Chapter 8

Safe Harbour Limit u/s 43CA, 50C and 56 of the Income Tax Act

8.1 Increase in Safe Harbour Limit u/s 43CA, 50C and 56 of the Income Tax Act from existing 5% to 10%

The Finance Bill 2020 has increased the safe harbour limit for stamp duty valuation based on circle rates u/s 43CA, 50C & 56 of the Income-tax Act, from existing 5% to 10%, w.e.f. AY 2021-22 and onwards.

In simple words, now, if the declared sale consideration towards land, building & house property, in sale deed, is less than corresponding circle rates of such properties and such shortfall is uptill 10%, then no addition u/s 43CA, 50C & 56 can be made, w.e.f. AY 2021-22 and onwards.

8.2 But is this increase to 10% in safe harbour limit, in current times of sluggishness in real-estate sector, when circles rates of properties are even higher than actual transaction rates, in many regions, enough?

To get an answer to this crucial question, it will be desirable and worthwhile to answer another question as to:

"Are Sections 50C/43CA/56(2) of Income Tax Act Resulting in Double Taxation & Contrary to Real Income Theory?"

The Finance Act 2002 has introduced a new section 50C with effect from 1-4-2003, for the purpose of computation of capital gains in real estate transactions, in the hands of seller of such land and/or building. Under this section the sale consideration as declared by the seller of land and/or building is to be substituted by the stamp duty valuation rate/circle rate of such land and/or building, in cases where the declared sale consideration is less than the corresponding stamp duty valuation rate/circle rate, for the purpose of calculating capital gains under Section 48 of the Income-tax Act, 1961.

Similarly a new section 43CA has been incorporated in the Income Tax Act by the Finance Act, 2013. Under this section the sale consideration as declared by the seller of land and/or building is to be substituted by the stamp duty valuation rates/circle rates of such land and/or building, in cases where the declared sale consideration is less than the corresponding stamp duty valuation rates/circle rates, for the purpose of calculating income in the hands of seller under the head "Profits & Gains of Business or Profession".

Since then, the Revenue Authorities are pressing into service the deeming fiction of substituting the declared sales consideration of land and/or building, by the stamp duty valuation rate/circle rate u/s 50C/43CA of the Act, and are re-computing the resultant capital gains/business gains respectively, on such deeming fiction basis, in the hands of the seller of such land and/or building.

Interestingly, the deeming fiction of taxability as envisaged in sections 50C and 43CA of the Income Tax Act, did not remain confined to just in the hands of seller of land and/or building and it has got extended in the hands of purchaser of land and/or building as well. There is one another section viz. 56(2)(*vii*)/56(2)(*x*) of the Income Tax Act, which provides for taxing the shortfall in the declared purchase consideration with that of the corresponding stamp duty valuation rate/circle rate of land and/or building in the hands of purchaser under the head 'income for other sources'.

Up till 1.4.2017, as per provisions of section 56(2)(*vii*), any sum of money or any property which was received without consideration or for inadequate consideration (in excess of the specified limit of Rs. 50,000) by an individual or HUF was chargeable to income-tax in the hands of the recipient under the head "Income from other sources". The definition of 'property' for the purpose of this section included immovable property, jewellery, shares, paintings, etc. The cases where the declared purchase consideration of land and/or building falls short of the corresponding stamp duty valuation rate/circle rate, were covered under the purview of the term 'inadequate consideration' in the context of receipt of an immovable property, by the purchaser.

The Finance Act, 2017 inserted a new clause (x) in sub-section (2) of section 56 so as to provide that receipt of the sum of money or the property by any person on or after 1-4-2017 without consideration or for inadequate consideration in excess of threshold limit of Rs. 50,000 shall be chargeable to tax in the hands of the recipient under the head "Income from other sources".

The Explanatory Memorandum to the Finance Bill, 2017 explained the rationale of the amendment as under:

"Widening scope of Income from Other Sources

Under the existing provisions of section 56(2)(vii), any sum of money or any property which is received without consideration or for inadequate consideration (in excess of the specified limit of Rs. 50,000) by an individual or HUF is chargeable to income-tax in the hands of the resident under the head "Income from other sources" subject to certain exceptions. Further, receipt of certain shares by a firm or a company in which the public are not substantially interested is also chargeable to income-tax in case such receipt is in excess of Rs. 50,000 and is received without consideration or for inadequate consideration. The existing definition of property for the purpose of this section includes immovable property, jewellery, shares, paintings, etc. These anti-abuse provisions are currently applicable only in case of individual or HUF and firm or company in certain cases. Therefore, receipt of sum of money or property without consideration or for inadequate consideration does not attract these anti-abuse provisions in cases of other assessees. In order to prevent the practice of receiving the sum of money or the property without consideration or for inadequate consideration, it is proposed to insert a new clause (x) in sub-section (2) of section 56 so as to provide that receipt of the sum of money or the property by any person without consideration or for inadequate consideration in excess of Rs. 50,000 shall be chargeable to tax in the hands of the recipient under the head "Income from other sources". It is also proposed to widen the scope of existing exceptions by including the receipt by certain trusts or institutions and receipt by way of certain transfers not regarded as transfer under section 47."

8.3 "Double Taxation"

In the existing framework of the Income Tax Act, for the same income or rather the deeming income, both the seller and the buyer of land and/or building, are being taxed twice and as such the pressing of service of such deeming fiction of taxation both in the hands of the seller and/or buyer of land and/or building is resulting in "Double Taxation". This 'double taxation' is contrary to the well-established and well settled principle of Law and canons of direct taxation that "a same income can't be taxed twice."

Time and again, numerous judgments of the Hon'ble Supreme Court and the Hon'ble High Courts have held the incidence and levy of 'double taxation' as unlawful and a nullity in the eyes of Law, prominent among these being the judgments of Hon'ble Supreme Court in the undermentioned cases viz.

(i)   *Laxmipat Singhania* v. *CIT* **[1969] 72 ITR 291 (SC)**

(ii)   *CIT* v. *Devi Prasad Vishwanath* **[1969] 72 ITR 194 (SC)**

The Legislature while preparing and legislating the Direct Taxation Laws has always kept in mind the unlawfulness and impermissibility of 'double taxation' of any particular income. The Income Tax Act contains numerous sections wherein the 'double taxation' of any income has been considered as impermissible and unlawful in the Act itself. The prominent examples include non-taxability of the partners' share of profits in the partnership firm/LLP, in the hands of partners by virtue of express exemption u/s. 10(2) of the Income Tax Act, non-taxability of Dividend income upto Rs. 10 lakhs, in the hands of recipient u/s. 115BBDA, the express provisions as contained in sections 90 and 91 of the Income Tax Act and the Double Taxation Avoidance Agreements (DTAA) ensuring the avoidance of double taxation of income in two countries.

No doubt, the Constitution of India does not curtails or prohibits the Legislature for enacting and incorporating the express and specific provisions in the Income Tax Act resulting in 'double taxation', as has been presently done in incorporating section 56(2)(vii)/56(2)(x) in the Act, in addition to the prevailing section 50C/43CA of the Income Tax Act.

However, it is also desirable to keep in mind that such imposition of 'double taxation' even by express provisions in the Act is principally and fundamentally contrary to the principles of natural justice, equity and fair play and as such must be avoided by the Legislature. Just as any particular expenditure is allowable as tax deductible expenditure only in the hands of one particular assessee only and it is not allowed in the hands of two or more assessees, similarly the same income can't be taxed twice in the hands of one or more assessees.

8.4 Contrary to "Real Income Theory"

Further, this deeming fiction of taxation as envisaged in sections 50C, 43CA and 56(2)(x) of the Income Tax Act, needs to be examined from another perspective also, that is the "real income theory" perspective.

Time and again, numerous judgments of the Hon'ble Supreme Court and the Hon'ble High Courts have upheld the "real income theory" postulating the taxation of only real and actual income and not notional income. Some of the significant judgments of Hon'ble Supreme Court in this regard are enumerated as under *viz.*

(*i*)   *CIT v. Shoorji Vallabhdas & Co.* **[1962] 46 ITR 144 (SC)**

(*ii*)   *CIT v. Chamanlal Mangaldas & Co.* **[1960] 39 ITR 8 (SC)**

(*iii*) *CIT v. Virtual Soft Systems Ltd.* **[2018] 92 taxmann.com 370/255 Taxman 352/404 ITR 409 (SC)**

(*iv*)   *CIT v. Bokaro Steel Ltd.* **[1999] 102 Taxman 94/236 ITR 315 (SC)**

In view of the currently prevailing sluggishness and slow-down in the real estate sector, the property transactions of sale and purchase of land and/or building, in majority regions and areas, are taking place at prices/rates much below their respective circle/stamp duty valuation rates.

In such cases, the application of the provisions of section 50C/43CA/56(2), deeming the sale/purchase consideration equivalent to the applicable stamp duty/circle rates irrespective of the fact that the actual sale/purchase consideration is lesser than the circle rate, is resulting in a lot of undue hardships both in the hands of sellers as well as buyers, in the form of unwarranted and unjustified income tax liability on notional sale/purchase consideration towards immovable property.

It needs to be appreciated that the legislative intent of introduction of the said sections 50C/43CA/56(2) was to plug the cash dealings and under-recording and reporting of sale/purchase consideration of immovable properties in the arena, wherein market rates of immovable properties were substantially higher than their corresponding circle rates.

However, presently times have changed. Circle Rates have been revised on a substantially higher side whereas the market rates of immovable properties have comparatively fallen in view of the sluggishness in the real estate sector, and as such the gap between the market rates and circle rates of immovable properties has narrowed down considerably and infact in large number of areas and regions, the actual transaction rates/market rates of immovable properties are even lower than the circle rates.

The well-established and well settled "real income theory" postulates that only real and actual income can be taxed and any notional income can't be brought under the purview of taxation. However, the existing legal provisions as contained in sections 50C, 43CA and 56(2)(x) of the Income Tax Act, provides for the deeming fiction of taxing the notional income in those cases of sale and/or purchase of land and/or building, where the actual transaction rates/market rates of such immovable properties are even lower than the circle rates.

The provision for reference to valuation officer u/s. 55A of the Act, in cases where the assessee objects to the adoption of stamp duty valuation rate/circle rate in deeming the sale/purchase consideration, is also practically turning out to be a redundant and ineffective provision in view of the subjectivity and complexity involved in such valuation.

8.5 Concluding remarks:

In view of the changed dynamics of the demand & supply conditions in the real estate sector, there is an immediate and crucial need for a further increase in the safe harbour limit u/s 43CA/50C/56(2) of the Act to atleast 25% from the existing 10%, so as to bring them in alignment with the actual transaction rates of immovable properties, in order to avoid the "taxation of notional income" contrary to the "real income theory" in order to provide the "ease of living" to the general masses and to provide the much needed push and fillip to the real estate sector.

Chapter 9

Incentives to Start-Ups

9. Amendments concerning Start-Ups in Finance Bill 2020

With a view to encourage and promote 'Start-ups', a slew of amendments has been made in the previous Budgets and even before the presenting of the Finance Bill 2020 in the Parliament.

The CBDT as per its Circular No. 22/2019 dated 30.8.2019, has stipulated the specified procedure in ongoing assessments of 'eligible start-ups' whose cases are under limited scrutiny on the single issue of applicability of section 56(2)(viib) (more popularly known as 'angel tax') and has provided that the contentions of such 'start-ups' in this regard, shall be summarily accepted.

9.1 Increase in the Qualifying Turnover Criteria & the Tax Holiday Period

The existing provisions of section 80-IAC of the Act provide for a deduction of an amount equal to one hundred per cent of the profits and gains derived from an eligible business by an eligible start-up for three consecutive assessment years out of seven years, at the option of the assessee, subject to the condition that the eligible start-up is incorporated on or after 1st April, 2016 but before 1st April, 2021 and the total turnover of its business does not exceed twenty-five crore rupees.

In order to further rationalise the provisions relating to start-ups, it is proposed to amend section 80-IAC of the Act so as to provide that-

(i) the deduction under the said section 80-IAC shall be available to an eligible start-up for a period of three consecutive assessment years out of ten years beginning from the year in which it is incorporated;

(ii) the deduction under the said section shall be available to an eligible start-up, if the total turnover of its business does not exceed one hundred crore rupees in any of the previous years beginning from the year in which it is incorporated.

This amendment will take effect from 1st April, 2021 and will, accordingly, apply in relation to the assessment year 2021-22 and subsequent assessment years.

9.2 Deferring TDS or tax payment in respect of income pertaining to Employee Stock Option Plan (ESOP) of start- ups.

ESOPs have been a significant component of the compensation for the employees of start-ups, as it allows the founders and start-ups to employ highly talented employees at a relatively low salary amount with balance being made up via ESOPs.

At present, when an employer allots shares to his employees under ESOP then the difference between the fair market value of shares on the date of exercising the option and the amount actually paid by the employee for such shares is taxable as perquisite under section 17(2)(vi) of the Income-tax Act and, consequently, employer is liable to include such perquisite in salary income of the employee and deduct tax thereon in the same year, i.e., the year in which shares are allotted.

Currently ESOPs are taxed as perquisites under section 17(2) of the Act read with Rule 3(8)(iii) of the Rules. The taxation of ESOPs is split into two components:

i. Tax on perquisite as income from salary at the time of exercise.

ii. Tax on income from capital gain at the time of sale.

The tax on perquisite is required to be paid at the time of exercising of option which may lead to cash flow problem as this benefit of ESOP is in kind.

In order to ease the burden of payment of taxes by the employees of the eligible start-ups or TDS deduction by the start-up employer, it has been proposed in the Finance Bill 2020 to amend section 192 of the Act, and insert sub-section (1C) therein to clarify that for the purpose of deducting or paying tax under sub-sections (1) or (1A) thereof, as the case may be, a person, being an eligible start-up referred to in section 80-IAC, responsible for paying any income to the assessee being perquisite of the nature specified in clause (vi) of sub-section (2) of section 17 of the Act, in any previous year relevant to the assessment year 2021-22 or subsequent assessment year, deduct or pay, as the case may be, tax on such income within fourteen days —

(i) after the expiry of forty-eight months from the end of the relevant assessment year; or

(ii) from the date of the sale of such specified security or sweat equity share by the assessee; or

(iii) from the date of which the assessee ceases to be the employee of the person;

whichever is the earliest on the basis of rates in force of the financial year in which the said specified security or sweat equity share is allotted or transferred.

Similar amendments have been carried out in section 191 (for assessee to pay the tax direct in case of no TDS) and in section 156 (for notice of demand) and in section 140A (for calculating self-assessment).

But, surprisingly, no corresponding amendment in relation to the deferment of tax incidence has been proposed in the charging section 17(2)(vi) which provides for chargeability of perquisite arising from ESOPs under the head 'salary'.

Thus, going by the existing amendments as above, perquisite arising from ESOPs shall be treated as income of an employee, for the year, in which shares are allotted but no tax would be required to be deducted or paid in that respect by the employer and employee, respectively.

However, it seems to be an inadvertent omission by the Legislature and as such needs to be addressed in a timely manner, so as to avoid any unnecessary confusion and uncertainty concerning the taxability of ESOPS in the hands of employees of Start-ups.

These amendments will take effect from 1st April, 2020.

9.3 Certain Ambiguities in the Amendments requiring further Clarity & Rationalisation

9.3.1 Need for Alignment of the Definition of 'Start-ups', in section 80IAC of the Income Tax Act and the Notification issued by DPIIT

As per section 80-IAC, an eligible start-up can only be a company or limited liability partnership (LLP) engaged in innovation, development or improvement of products or processes or services or a scalable business model with a high potential of employment generation or wealth creation.

Further, it has to satisfy the following conditions:

i. It must be incorporated on or after 01-04-2016 but before 31-03-2021;

ii. Total turnover shall not exceed Rs. 100 crores in the previous year for which deduction under section 80-IAC is claimed; and

iii. It must hold a certificate of eligible business from the Inter-Ministerial Board of Certification.

It is interesting to mention here that as on December 18, 2019, only **250 'start-ups'** have been recognised by the Inter-Ministerial Board of Certification.

The above two proposed amendments in section 80IAC of the Income Tax Act, concerning the increase in the qualifying turnover limit to Rs 100 crores from the existing Rs. 25 crores, and the increase in Tax Holiday Period availability to "3 consecutive years out of a period of 10 years from the incorporation of the start-up", from the existing, "3 consecutive years out of a period of 7 years from the incorporation of the start-up", are a very positive and welcome steps in the direction of alignment of the definition of 'Start-ups', in section 80IAC of the Income Tax Act and the Notification issued by DPIIT.

however, still, there are some unwanted and confusing mismatches between the two, which need to be addressed by the Law Makers.

For ready reference and benefit of worthy readers, a comparative analysis of the two pieces of legislation concerning 'Start-Ups', viz. section 80IAC and DPIIT Notification are summarised and tabulated below:

Particulars	Definition as per DPIIT	Definition as per section 80-IAC
Form/ Constitution	The start-up may be incorporated as a Company, LLP or a Partnership Firm.	The start-up may be incorporated as a Company or LLP only. Currently section 80IAC does not give recognition to a Partnership Firm as a Start-up.
Period of Incorporation	No stipulation as to the date of incorporation	Should be incorporated between 01-04-2016 and 31-03-2021

Nature of Business	Entity should be engaged in the business of innovation, development or improvement of products or processes or services, or if it is a scalable business model with a high potential of employment generation or wealth creation.	Entity should be engaged in the business of innovation, development or improvement of products or processes or services, or if it is a scalable business model with a high potential of employment generation or wealth creation.
Tax Holiday Period Window	An entity is considered as an eligible start-up up to a period of 10 years from the date of incorporation/registration	An entity is considered as an eligible start-up up to a period of 10 years from beginning from the year in which it is incorporated or registered
Turnover Threshold	Turnover of entity for any of the financial years since incorporation/registration should not exceed Rs. 100 crores	Turnover of entity for any of the financial years since incorporation/registration should not exceed Rs. 100 crores

Reorganization	The entity should not be formed by splitting up or reconstruction of an existing business	The entity should not be formed by splitting up or reconstruction of an existing business except in a situation specified in section 33B
Second-hand plant or machinery	No condition as to the status of plant or machinery purchased for the business	Value of second-hand plant and machinery should not exceed 20% of the total value of plant and machinery used in the business
Benefit of deferment of TDS on perquisites arising from ESOPs	Not allowed	Allowed

Chapter 10

Abolition of Corporate Dividend Distribution Tax (DDT)

10.1 Going Back to the Classical System of Taxing Dividends in the hands of Recipients

At present, a domestic company is liable to pay DDT under section 115-O on any dividend distributed by it to the shareholders. Consequently, shareholders are exempt from paying tax on such dividend income by virtue of section 10(34). However, when a resident shareholder (other than a domestic company, educational institute or hospitals as referred to in clauses (iv) to (via) of Section 10(23C) or a trust registered under section 12A/12AA) gets dividend from the domestic company in excess of Rs. 10 lakhs, such excess dividend is taxable under Section 115BBDA at the rate of 10%*plus* applicable surcharge and health & education cess. This additional tax under Section 115BBDA is levied on all types of dividends except deemed dividend as referred to in Section 2(22)(e), i.e., loans or advance to the shareholders.

The existing provisions concerning the levy of tax on dividend income are resulting in taxation at four levels viz.

(a) firstly, as regular corporate income tax on corporate profits;

(b) secondly, as DDT in the hands of corporate entities;

(c) thirdly, as tax on dividends in the hands of recipients u/s115BBDA, if the dividend income exceeds Rs. 10,00,000/- p.a.;

(d) fourthly, as disallowance u/s 14A w.r.t. dividend income.

Thus, there was an urgent and dire need to eliminate this unjustified cascading of taxes and the scrapping of DDT in the hands of corporate entities.

Accordingly, it has been proposed to go back to the classical system of taxing dividend income so that dividend or income from units are taxable in the hands of shareholders or unit holders at the applicable rate and the domestic company or specified company or mutual funds are not required to pay any DDT.

It has also been proposed to provide that the deduction for expense under section 57 of the Act shall be maximum 20 per cent of the dividend or income from units.

10.2 Proposed Amendments in Finance Bill 2020

The Finance Bill 2020 has proposed to-

(i)   amend section 115-O to provide that dividend declared, distributed or paid after 1st April, 2003, but on or before 31st March, 2020 shall be covered under the provision of this section.

(ii)   amend clause (34) of section 10 to provide that the provision of this clause shall not apply to any income, by way of dividend, received on or after 1st April, 2020.

(iii)   amend section 115R to provide that the income distributed on or before 31st March, 2020 shall only be covered under the provision of this section.

(iv)   amend clause (35) of section 10 to provide that the provision of this clause shall not apply to any income, in respect of units, received on or after 1st April, 2020.

(v) amend clause (23FC) of section 10 so that all dividends received or receivable by business trust from a special purpose vehicle is exempt income under this clause.

(vi) amend clause (23FD) of section 10 to exclude dividend income received by a unit holder from business trust from the exemption so that the dividend income is taxable in the hand of unit holder of the business trust.

(vii) amend sub-section (3) of section 115UA to delete reference to sub-clause (a) so that distributed income of the nature as referred to in clause (23FC) or clause (23FCA) of section 10 shall be deemed to be income of the unit holder and shall be charged to tax as income of the previous year. Thus, dividend income distributed by a special purpose vehicle to business trust would be taxed in the hands of unit holder.

(viii) remove reference of section 115-O dividend income in various sections like section 57, section 115A, section 115AC, section 115ACA, section 115AD and section 115C.

(ix) remove the opening line of clause (23D) of section 10, as mutual fund no longer required to pay additional tax.

(x) insert new section 80M as it existed before it removal by the Finance Act, 2003 to remove the cascading affect, with a change that set off will be allowed only for dividend distributed by the company one month prior to the due date of filing of return, in place of due date of filing return earlier.

(xi) amend section 115BBDA which taxes dividend income in excess of ten lakh rupee in the hands of shareholder at ten per cent., to only dividend declared, distributed or paid by a domestic company on or before the 31st day of March, 2020.

(xii) amend section 57 to provide that no deduction shall be allowed from dividend income, or income in respect of units of mutual fund or specified company, other than deduction on account of interest expense and in any previous year such deduction shall not exceed twenty per cent. of the dividend income or income from units included in the total income for that year without deduction under section 57.

(xiii) amend section 194 to include dividend for tax deduction. At the same time the rates of ten per cent. is proposed to be prescribed and threshold is proposed to be increased from Rs 2,500/- to Rs 5,000/- for dividend paid other than cash. Further, at present the mode of payment is given as "an account payee cheque or warrant". It is proposed to change this to any mode.

(xiv) amend section 194LBA to provide for tax deduction by business trust on dividend income paid to unit holder, at the rate of ten per cent. for resident. For non-resident, it would be 5 per cent for interest and ten per cent. for dividend.

(xv) insert a new section 194K to provide that any person responsible for paying to a resident any income in respect of units of a Mutual Fund specified under clause (23D) of section 10 or units from the administrator of the specified undertaking or units from the specified company shall at the time of credit of such income to the account of the payee or at the time of payment thereof by any mode, whichever is earlier, deduct income-tax there on at the rate of ten per cent. It may also be provided for threshold limit of Rs 5,000/- so that income below this amount does not suffer tax deduction. It is also proposed to defined "Administrator", "specified company", as already defined in clause (35) of section 10. It is also proposed to define "specified undertaking" as in clause (i) of section 2 of the Unit Trust of India

(Transfer of Undertaking and Repeal) Act, 2002. It is also proposed to provide that where any income is credited to any account like suspense account, in the books of account of the person liable to pay such income, the liability for tax deduction under this section would arise at that time.

(xvi) amend section 195 to delete exemption provided to dividend referred to in section 115-O.

(xvii) amend section 196A to revive its applicability on TDS on income in respect of units of a Mutual Fund. It is also proposed to substitute "of the Unit Trust of India" with "from the specified company defined in Explanation to clause (35) of section 10" and "in cash or by the issue of a cheque or draft or by any other mode" with "by any mode".

(xviii) amend section 196C to remove exclusion provided to dividend under section 115-O. It is also proposed to substitute "in cash or by the issue of a cheque or draft or by any other mode" with "by any mode".

(xix) amend section 196D to remove exclusion provided to dividend under section 115-O. It is also proposed to substitute "in cash or by the issue of a cheque or draft or by any other mode" with "by any mode".

Amendments at clause (i) to (xii) above will take effect from 1st April, 2021 and will, accordingly, apply in relation to the AY 2021-22 and subsequent assessment years. Amendments at clause (xiii) to (xix) will take effect from 1st April, 2020.

10.3 Impact Analysis of Proposed Amendments

10.3.1 Foreign investors

Removal of DDT regime shall be beneficial for the foreign investors as it will minimize tax cost of investment in India and credit of such tax cost would be available in their home country. However, in respect of foreign investors being discretionary trust and AOP, rate of tax applicable may be the maximum marginal rate, which shall be substantially higher than tax rate for foreign companies, unless treaty benefits are available.

10.3.2 Domestic Investors

i) Domestic Companies

a) Before Amendment (uptill AY 2020-21)

The domestic companies paying dividends were required to pay Dividend Distribution Tax (DDT) at an effective rate of 20.56%.

However, no tax was payable on dividend income being received by domestic companies.

b) Post Amendment (w.e.f. AY 2021-22)

In case of domestic companies, receiving dividends, tax @ rate of 30% plus applicable surcharge in old corporate tax regime and tax @ 22%/15% plus applicable surcharge in the new corporate tax regime u/s 115BAA and 115BAB, shall be levied on the dividend income being received by them.

However, no DDT is payable by the domestic companies at the time of payment of dividends.

ii). Individual Investors

a) Before Amendment (uptill AY 2020-21)

Uptill AY 2020-21, dividend income up to Rs. 10 lakhs was exempt, in the hands of recipient shareholders and dividend income in excess of Rs 10 lakhs was taxable in the hands of recipient shareholders at a special rate of 10% u/s 115BBDA.

Case Study on Tax Liability on Dividend Income Before Amendment (uptill AY 2020-21)

(Amount in INR Lakhs)

Assessee	Income Levels (excluding Dividend)	Applicable Tax Rate (%) *	Dividend Income (Exempt u/s 10(34)	Tax on Total Income	Tax on Dividend Income u/s 115BBDA @ 10%	Total tax Liability
P	7.50	10	2.5	0.75	0	0.75
Q	10.00	20	5.00	2.00	0	2.00
R	15.00	30	10.00	4.50	0	4.50
S	20.00	30	15.00	6.00	1.50	7.50

*Personal Tax Rates under Old Regime have been Considered and surcharge and education cess have been ignored for simplicity & better understanding.

b) After Amendment (w.e.f. AY 2021-22)

W.e.f. AY 2021-22, in case of domestic individual investors, receiving dividends, tax at their applicable slab rates shall be levied on dividend income being received by them. However, no special tax u/s 115BBDA would be levied.

Case Study on Tax Liability on Dividend Income Before Amendment (uptill AY 2020-21)

(Amount in INR Lakhs)

Assessee	Income Levels (excluding Dividend)	Dividend Income (not exempt u/s 10(34)	Total Income	Applicable Tax Rate (%) *	Tax on Dividend Income u/s 115BBDA @ 10%	Total tax Liability
P	7.50	2.5	10.00	20	0	2.00
Q	10.00	5.00	15.00	30	0	4.50
R	15.00	10.00	25.00	30	0	7.50
S	20.00	15.00	35.00	30	0	10.50

*Personal Tax Rates under Old Regime have been Considered and surcharge and education cess have been ignored for simplicity & better understanding.

Comparison between Pre & Post Amendment Scenario w.r.t. Taxability of Dividend Income in the Hands of Individual Recipient Shareholders

(Amount in INR Lakhs)

Assessee	Pre-Amendment Ta Liability	Post Amendment Tax Liability	Net Savings/ (Loss)
P	0.75	2.00	(1.25)
Q	2.00	4.50	(1.50)
R	4.50	7.50	(3.00)
S	7.50	10.50	(3.00)

Conclusion: It is duly evident from above comparative analysis, that in the post amendment period w.e.f. AY 2021-22, since the dividend income being received by individual recipient shareholders, will not be considered as exempt income u/s 10(34), and will be considered as taxable income, thus, such dividend income will result in an increase in tax slab rates of individual recipient shareholders, and as such will result in more tax liability vis-à-vis the pre-amendment regime, even after taking into consideration the removal of special tax rate of 10% on dividend incomes in excess of Rs. 10 lakhs u/s 115BBDA.

10.3.3 Obligation of the Domestic Companies paying Dividend

The domestic companies shall not be liable to pay DDT on dividend distributed to shareholders on or after 01-04-2020. However, domestic companies shall be liable to deduct tax under Section 194. The Finance Bill, 2020 has also proposed amendments to Section 194.

As per the amended Section 194, which shall be applicable to dividend distributed, declared or paid on or after 01-04-2020, an Indian company shall deduct tax at the rate of 10% from dividend distributed to the resident shareholders if the aggregate amount of dividend distributed or paid during the financial year to a shareholder exceeds Rs. 5,000. However, no tax shall be required to be deducted from the dividend paid or payable to Life Insurance Corporation of India (LIC), General Insurance Corporation of India (GIC) or any other insurer in respect of any shares owned by it or in which it has full beneficial interest.

The proposed amendments providing for deduction of TDS @ 10% u/s 194, on dividend income received by individuals and HUFs in excess of Rs. 5000, may create difficulties for such assessees, in the form of increased compliance burdens of filing their ITRs, in order to claim the refund of the TDS being deducted on their dividend incomes, if they are in the exempt slab of income tax.

Where the dividend is payable to a non-resident or a foreign company, the tax shall be deducted under Section 195 in accordance with the relevant Double Taxation Avoidance Agreements (DTAAs).

a. Withholding Tax on Dividend Income as per DTAAs

The dividend income in the hands of foreign investors in Indian Domestic Companies shall be taxable in India as per the provisions of the Income Tax Act or as per relevant DTAA, whichever is more beneficial, to the assessee.

Dividend income is generally chargeable to tax in the source country as well as the country of residence of the assessee and, consequently, country of residence provides a credit of taxes paid by the assessee in the source country.

As per most of the DTAAs India has entered into with foreign countries, the dividend is taxable in the source country in the hands of the beneficial owner of shares at the rate ranging from 5% to 15% of the gross amount of the dividends.

b. Possibility of Dividend Stripping arising out of DTAA

In DTAA with countries like Canada, Denmark, Singapore, the dividend tax rate is further reduced where the dividend is payable to a company which holds specific percentage (generally 25%) of shares of the company paying the dividend. However, no minimum time limit has been prescribed in these DTAAs for which such shareholding should be maintained by the recipient company. Therefore, MNCs were often found misusing the provisions by increasing their shareholding in the company declaring immediately before declaration of the dividend and offloading the same after getting the dividend.

India did not face this situation as dividend income was exempt from tax in the hands of the shareholders. However, after the proposed amendment, India too will face the risk of tax avoidance by the foreign company by artificially increasing the holding in the dividend declarant domestic company.

India is a signatory to the Multilateral Convention (MLI) which shall implement the measures recommended by the OECD to prevent Base Erosion and Profit Shifting. MLI is a binding international legal instrument which is envisaged with a view to swiftly implement the measures recommended by OECD to prevent Base Erosion and Profit Shifting in existing bilateral tax treaties in force. With respect to dividend income, Article 8 (Dividend Transfer Transactions) of MLI provides for a minimum period of 365 days for which a shareholder, receiving dividend income, has to maintain its shareholding in the company paying the dividend to get the benefit of the reduced tax rate on the dividend.

As the taxability of dividend is proposed to be shifted from companies to shareholders, the Government has proposed to introduce a new section 80M under the Act to remove the cascading effect where a domestic company receives a dividend from another domestic company. However, nothing has been prescribed where a domestic company receives dividend from a foreign company and further distribute the same to its shareholders. The taxability in such cases shall be as under:

10.3.4. Inter Corporate Dividend

a. Domestic Company receiving Dividend Income from another Domestic Company

As the taxability of dividend is proposed to be shifted from companies to shareholders, the

Government has proposed to re-introduce section 80M under the Act to remove the cascading effect where a domestic company receives a dividend from another domestic company.

Where a domestic company receives dividend from another domestic company, a new section 80M has been proposed to be inserted. This provision removes the cascading effect by providing that inter-corporate dividend shall be reduced from total income of company receiving the dividend if same is further distributed to shareholders one month prior to the due date of filing of return.

b. **Domestic Company receiving Dividend Income from a Foreign Company**

In the Finance Bill 2020, nothing has been prescribed where a domestic company receives dividend from a foreign company and further distribute the same to its shareholders.

The taxability of the dividend income in such cases as per existing provisions under the Income Tax Act, is as under:

Dividend received by a domestic company from a foreign company, in which such domestic company has 26% or more equity shareholding, is taxable at a rate of 15% *plus* Surcharge and Health and Education

Cess under Section 115BBD. Such tax shall be computed on a gross basis without allowing deduction for any expenditure.

Dividend received by a domestic company from a foreign company, in which equity shareholding of such domestic company is less than 26%, is taxable at normal tax rate. The domestic company can claim deduction for any expense incurred by it for the purposes of earning such dividend income.

The Hon'ble FM in her Budget Speech have mentioned that the abolition of Dividend Distribution will lead to estimated annual revenue forgone of Rs. 25,000 Crore.

However, in view of the fact that earlier the companies were subject to the levy of DDT at an effective tax rate of 20.56%, and currently, after this amendment, the High Networth Individuals (HNIs) may be subject to a maximum marginal tax rate of as high as 42.74% (including surcharge), this figure of estimated revenue foregone, appears to be doubtful.

Chapter 11

Increase in Turnover Threshold Limit for Tax Audits u/s 44AB

11.1 Proposed Amendment in Finance Bill 2020

Under section 44AB of the Act, every person carrying on business is required to get his accounts audited, if his total sales, turnover or gross receipts, in business exceed or exceeds one crore rupees in any previous year. In case of a person carrying on profession he is required to get his accounts audited, if his gross receipt in profession exceeds, fifty lakh rupees in any previous year.

In order to reduce compliance burden on small and medium enterprises, it is proposed to increase the threshold limit for a person carrying on business from one crore rupees to five crore rupees in cases where-

(i)   aggregate of all receipts in cash during the previous year does not exceed five per cent of such receipt; and

(ii) aggregate of all payments in cash during the previous year does not exceed five per cent of such payment.

Further, to enable pre-filling of returns in case of persons having income from business or profession, it is required that the tax audit report may be furnished by the said assessees at least one month prior to the due date of filing of return of income. This requires amendments in all the sections of the Act which mandates filing of audit report along with the return of income or by the due date of filing of return of income. Thus, provisions of section 10, section 10A, section 12A, section 32AB, section 33AB, section 33ABA, section 35D, section 35E, section 44AB, section 44DA, section 50B, section 80-IA, section 80-IB, section 80JJAA, section 92F, section 115JB, section 115JC and section 115VW of the Act are proposed to be amended accordingly.

Further, the due date for filing return of income under sub-section (1) of section 139 is proposed to be amended by:

(A) providing 31st October of the assessment year (as against 30th September) as the due date for an assessee referred to in clause (a) of Explanation 2 of sub-section (1) of Section 139 of the Act;

(B) removing the distinction between a working and a non-working partner of a firm with respect to the due date as mentioned in sub-clause (iii) of clause (a) of Explanation 2 of sub-section (1) of Section 139 of the Act.

These amendments will take effect from 1st April, 2020 and will, accordingly, apply in relation to the assessment year 2020-21 and subsequent assessment years.

The amendment relating to extending threshold for getting books of accounts audited will have consequential effect on TDS/TCS provisions contained in sections 194A, 194C, 194H, 194I, 194J and 206C as these provisions fasten liability of TDS/TCS on certain categories of person, if the gross receipt or turnover from the business or profession carried on by them exceed the monetary limit specified in clause (a) or clause (b) of section 44AB.

Therefore, it is proposed to amend these sections so that reference to the monetary limit specified in clause (a) or clause (b) of section 44AB of the Act is substituted with rupees one crore in case of the business or rupees fifty lakh in case of the profession, as the case may be.

These amendments will take effect from 1st April, 2020.

11.2 Conclusions

Therefore, the Finance Bill 2020 has proposed to increase the turnover threshold limit for the Tax Audits u/s 44AB, for the persons carrying on business, to Rs. 5 crores from the existing Rs.1 crore, in all those cases where, the aggregate annual cash receipts and cash payments, do not exceed 5% of their total receipts and payments respectively.

It is noteworthy here that the terminology aggregate annual cash receipts and cash payments in the case of the assessees following mercantile system of accounting, should be construed as the aggregate annual cash receipts and cash payments, being recognised as revenue and expenditure in their books of accounts as per mercantile system of accounting only and not on the basis of cash system of accounting.

Further, the turnover thresholds for deduction of TDS/TCS u/s 194A, 194C, 194H, 194I, 194J and 206C, have been continued to remain the same viz. Rs 1 crore only and not Rs. 5 crores.

The due dates for filing of ITRs in all the Tax Auditable Cases, has also been extended to 31st October from the existing date of 30th September of the following financial year.

Further, the existing threshold limit of Rs 50 lakhs for the tax audits, for persons carrying on profession has also not been increased.

Chapter 12

TDS on e-Commerce Transactions

12.1 Insertion of New Section 194-O for Levy of TDS @ 1% on E-Commerce Transactions

In order to widen and deepen the tax net by bringing participants of e-commerce within tax net, the Finance Bill 2020 has proposed to insert a new section 194-O in the Act so as to provide for a new levy of TDS at the rate of one per cent, with the following key points:

- The TDS is to be paid by e-commerce operator for sale of goods or provision of service facilitated by it through its digital or electronic facility or platform;

- E-commerce operator is required to deduct tax at the time of credit of amount of sale or service or both to the account of e-commerce participant or at the time of payment thereof to such participant by any mode, whichever is earlier.

- The tax at one per cent is required to be deducted on the gross amount of such sales or service or both.

- Any payment made by a purchaser of goods or recipient of services directly to an e-commerce participant shall be deemed to be amount credited or paid by the e-commerce operator to the e-commerce participant and shall be included in the gross amount of such sales or services for the purpose of deduction of income-tax.

- The sum credited or paid to an e-commerce participant (being an individual or HUF) by the e-commerce operator shall not be subjected to provision of this section, if the gross amount of sales or services or both of such individual or HUF, through e-commerce operator, during the previous year does not exceed five lakh rupees and such e-commerce participant has furnished his Permanent Account Number (PAN) or Aadhaar number to the e-commerce operator.

- A transaction in respect of which tax has been deducted by the e-commerce operator under this section or which is not liable to deduction under the exemption discussed in the previous bullet, there shall not be further liability on that transaction for TDS under any other provision of Chapter XVII-B of the Act. This is to provide clarity so that same transaction is not subjected to TDS more than once. However, it has been clarified that this exemption will not apply to any amount received or receivable by an e-commerce operator for hosting advertisements or providing any other services which are not in connection with the sale of goods or services referred to in sub-section (1) of the proposed section.

- "e-commerce operator" is defined to mean any person who owns, operates or manages digital or electronic facility or platform for electronic commerce and is a person responsible for paying to e-commerce participant.

- "e-commerce participant" is defined to mean a person resident in India selling goods or providing services or both, including digital products, through digital or electronic facility or platform for electronic commerce.

- "electronic commerce" is defined to mean the supply of goods or services or both, including digital products, over digital or electronic network.

- "services" is defined to include fees for technical services and fees for professional services, as defined in section 194J.

- Consequential amendments are being proposed in section 197 (for lower TDS), in section 204 (to define person responsible for paying any sum) and in section 206AA (to provide for tax deduction at 5 per cent in non-PAN/ Aadhaar cases).

This amendment will take effect from 1st April, 2020.

12.2 Explaining the Newly Inserted Provision of Deduction of TDS u/s 194O with Examples

a. Shashank, (recipient of services), a tax practitioner, orders his favourite pepe paneer pizza of Dominos (e-commerce participant), on Zomato (e-commerce operator) and makes the online payment of Rs. 300/-.

In this e-commerce transaction, the payment of Rs. 300/- being made by an individual Shashank, (recipient of services), directly to Dominos (e-commerce participant), shall be deemed to be amount credited or paid by Zomato (e-commerce operator) to Dominos (e-commerce participant) and shall be included in the gross amount of such sales or services for the purpose of deduction of income-tax. Dominos, furnishes its PAN/Aadhar Card to Zomato.

Zomato (e-commerce operator), shall be required to deduct TDS of Rs. 3/- @ 1 % u/s 194O, on Rs. 300/-, and deposit the said amount of TDS with the Exchequer, just like any other TDS and Dominos (e-commerce participant) can claim the credit of this TDS u/s 194O in its Return of Income.

b. On another day, being conscious about his junk diet, Shashank orders a 'Home Thali' from 'Homely Kitchen' a brand listed by Ms Arti (an individual e-commerce participant, having her annual sales of Rs. 5 lakhs from her brand 'Homely Kitchen' listed on Swiggy (e-commerce operator) and makes the payment of Rs 300/-.

Swiggy (e-commerce operator), shall be required to deduct TDS of Rs. 3/- @ 1 % u/s 194O, on Rs. 300/-, and deposit the said amount of TDS with the Exchequer, just like any other TDS.

It is pertinent to mention here that TDS @ 1% is applicable only, if Ms Arti furnishes her PAN/Aadhar Card Number. In the absence of PAN/Aadhar Card Number the rate of TDS deduction shall be 5%.

Further, if Ms Arti's gross annual sales from her brand of 'Homely Kitchen' listed on Swiggy, are Rs 4 lakhs (less than the prescribed threshold of Rs. 5 lakhs, in case of an individual/HUF e-commerce participant'), then Swiggy shall not deduct any TDS u/s 194O of the Act.

Chapter 13

Tax treatment of Employer's Contribution to Recognized Provident Funds, Superannuation Funds and National Pension Scheme

13.1 Proposed Amendment in Finance Bill 2020

The Finance Bill 2020 has proposed to provide a combined upper limit of seven lakh and fifty thousand rupees in respect of employer's contribution in a year to National Pension Scheme (NPS), superannuation fund and recognised provident fund and any excess contribution is proposed to be taxable.

It has also been proposed that any annual accretion by way of interest, dividend or any other amount of similar nature during the previous year to the balance at the credit of the fund or scheme may be treated as perquisite to the extent it relates to the employer's contribution which is included in total income.

13.2 Rationale & Objective of the Proposed Amendment

The Memorandum to Finance Bill 2020, explaining the rationale and objective of the said proposed amendment, reads as under:

"Under the existing provisions of the Act, the contribution by the employer to the account of an employee in a recognized provident fund exceeding twelve per cent of salary is taxable.

Further, the amount of any contribution to an approved superannuation fund by the employer exceeding one lakh fifty thousand rupees is treated as perquisite in the hands of the employee.

Similarly, the assessee is allowed a deduction under National Pension Scheme (NPS) for the fourteen per cent of the salary contributed by the Central Government and ten per cent of the salary contributed by any other employer.

However, there is no combined upper limit for the purpose of deduction on the amount of contribution made by the employer.

This is giving undue benefit to employees earning high salary income. While an employee with low salary income is not able to let employer contribute a large part of his salary to all these three funds, employees with high salary income are able to design their salary package in a manner where a large part of their salary is paid by the employer in these three funds.

Thus, this portion of salary does not suffer taxation at any point of time, since Exempt-Exempt-Exempt (EEE) regime is followed for these three funds. Thus, not having a combined upper cap is iniquitous and hence, not desirable.

Therefore, it is proposed to provide a combined upper limit of seven lakh and fifty thousand rupees in respect of employer's contribution in a year to NPS, superannuation fund and recognised provident fund and any excess contribution is proposed to be taxable.

Consequently, it is also proposed that any annual accretion by way of interest, dividend or any other amount of similar nature during the previous year to the balance at the credit of the fund or scheme may be treated as perquisite to the extent it relates to the employer's contribution which is included in total income."

This amendment will take effect from 1st April, 2021 and will, accordingly, apply in relation to the AY 2021-22 and subsequent assessment years.

Chapter 14

Incentives to Resident Co-operative Societies

14.1 The Taxation Laws (Amendment) Act, 2019, (TLAA), sought to provide additional fiscal stimulus to attract investment, generate employment and boost the economy in the wake of economic developments post enactment of the Finance (No. 2) Act, 2019 and keeping in view the reduction of rate of corporate income tax by many countries world over. TLAA, *inter alia*, introduced section 115BAA in the Act so as to provide that an existing domestic company may opt to pay tax at 22 per cent., if it does not claim any incentive and deduction as provided in said section.

In case of the domestic company opting to pay tax at the rate of 22 per cent. under said section, it was provided that-

(a) failure to satisfy specified conditions would disqualify it for the concessional rate and normal provisions of the Act shall apply.

(b) deemed loss or depreciation arising out of amalgamation

attributable to any incentive, deduction or exemption, shall not be allowed in computation of income.

(c) for FY 2020-21, where there is unabsorbed depreciation allowance in respect of a block of asset which has not been given full effect to in earlier FYs, corresponding adjustment shall be made to the written down value of such block of assets as on 1st April, 2020.

(d) it shall be entitled to deduction under section 80LA of the Act, subject to fulfilment of conditions contained therein, in respect of a Unit in the International Financial Services Centre, if any.

It was also provided that such company shall not be subjected to Minimum Alternate Tax (MAT) under section 115JB of the Act and that, the carry forward and set off of MAT credit, if any, under section 115JAA of the Act would not be allowed.

Representations have been received from the stakeholders requesting to provide for concessional rate of tax in case of resident co-operative society on similar lines. In view of the above, it is proposed to insert a new section (115BAD) in the Act to provide that-

(i) notwithstanding anything contained in the Act but subject to the provisions of Chapter XII and satisfaction of certain conditions, a co-operative society resident in India shall have the option to pay tax at 22 per cent. for assessment year 2021-22 onwards in respect of its total income so however that if it fails to satisfy the conditions in any previous year, the option shall become invalid and other provisions of the Act shall apply;

(ii) the condition for concessional rate shall be that the total income of the co-operative society is computed —

(a) without any deduction under the provisions of section 10AA or clause (iia) of sub-section (1) of section 32 or section 32AD or section 33AB or section 33ABA or sub-clause (ii) or sub-clause (iia) or sub-clause (iii) of sub-section (1) or sub-section (2AA) of section 35 or section 35AD or section 35CCC or under any provisions of Chapter VI-A;

(b) without set off of any loss carried forward or depreciation from any earlier assessment year, if such loss or depreciation is attributable to any of the deductions referred to in (a) above; and

(c) by claiming the depreciation, if any, under section 32, except clause (iia) of sub-section (1) thereof, determined in such manner as may be prescribed;

(iii) the loss and depreciation referred to in (ii)(b) above shall be deemed to have been given full effect to and no further deduction for such loss or depreciation shall be allowed for any subsequent year. However, where there is a depreciation allowance in respect of a block of asset which has not been given full effect to prior to the assessment year beginning on 1st April, 2021, corresponding adjustment shall be made to the written down value of such block of assets as on 1st April, 2020 in the prescribed manner, if the option is exercised for a previous year relevant to the assessment year beginning on 1st April, 2021;

(iv) the concessional rate shall not apply unless option is exercised by the co-operative society in the prescribed manner on or before the due date specified under sub-section (1) of section 139 of the Act for furnishing the returns of income for any previous year relevant to the assessment year commencing on or after 1st April, 2021 and such option once exercised shall apply to subsequent assessment years;

(v) if the person has a Unit in the International Financial Services Centre (IFSC), as referred to in sub-section (1A) of section 80LA, the deduction under section 80LA shall be available to such Unit subject to fulfilment of the conditions contained in that section; and

(vi)   the option so exercised cannot be withdrawn;

(vii)   The surcharge applicable to such co-operative society shall be levied at 10 per cent.

It is further proposed to amend section 115JC of the Act so as to provide that the provisions relating to Alternate Minimum Tax (AMT) shall not apply to such co-operative society.

It is also proposed to amend section 115JD of the Act so as to provide that the provisions relating to carry forward and set off of AMT credit, if any, shall not apply to such co-operative society.

This amendment will take effect from 1st April, 2021 and will, accordingly, apply in relation to the AY 2021-22 and subsequent assessment years.

Chapter 15

UPSC Chairman & Members & Chief Election Commissioners & Election Commissioners Brought under Income Tax Net

15.1 Withdrawal of exemption on certain perquisites or allowances provided to Union Pubic Services Commission (UPSC) Chairman and members and Chief Election Commissioner and Election Commissioners

Section 10 of the Act provides for exemption in respect of certain incomes and activities under specific circumstances. Clause (45) thereof, inserted by the Finance Act, 2011, provides that any allowance or perquisite as may be notified by the Central Government, paid to the serving/ retired Chairman or Members of UPSC shall not be included in computing their total income and hence shall be exempt from income-tax.

Further, vide Notification No. 49/2011 dated 6th September, 2011 bearing SO 2045(E), it was notified that in the case of serving Chairman and members of UPSC the following allowances and perquisites shall be exempt from income-tax for the purposes of clause (45) of section 10 of the Act, with effect from 1st April, 2008:

(i) the value of rent-free official residence;

(ii) the value of conveyance facilities including transport allowance;

(iii) the sumptuary allowance;

(iv) the value of leave travel concession provided to a serving Chairman or member of the UPSC and members of his family.

In the case of retired Chairman and members of UPSC, the said Notification states that the following allowances and perquisites shall be exempt from income-tax for the purposes of clause (45) of section 10 of the Act, with effect from 1st April, 2008:

(i) a sum of maximum of Rs 14,000 per month for defraying the service of an orderly and for meeting expenses incurred towards secretarial assistance on contract basis;

(ii) the value of a residential telephone free of cost and the number of free calls to the extent of 1500 per month (overall and above the number of free calls per month allowed by telephone authorities).

Section 8 of the Election Commission (Conditions of Service of Election Commissioners and Transaction of Business) Act, 1991 which determines the conditions of service of the Chief Election Commissioner and other Election Commissioners, provides for income-tax exemption to the Chief Election Commissioner and other Election Commissioners on the value of rent-free residence, conveyance facilities, sumptuary allowance, medical facilities and other such conditions of service as are applicable to a Judge of the Supreme Court under Chapter IV of the Supreme Court Judges (Conditions of Service) Act, 1958 and the rules made thereunder.

It is proposed to remove these exemptions. Accordingly, it proposed to:

(i) delete cause (45) of section 10 of the Act;

(ii) amend section 8 of the Election Commission (Conditions of Service of Election Commissioners and Transaction of Business) Act, 1991, so as to delete the exemption from income-tax on value of rent-free residence, conveyance facilities, sumptuary allowance, medical facilities and other such conditions of service as are applicable to a Judge of the Supreme Court, paid to Chief Election Commissioner and other Election Commissioners.

These amendments will take effect from 1st April, 2021 and will, accordingly, apply in relation to the assessment year 2021-22 and subsequent assessment years.

Chapter 16

International Taxation

16. The global tax landscape has been witnessing exponential changes, with tax administrations around the world continuously gearing up to keep pace with the rapid technological advancements to ramp up the effectiveness of their tax administrations.

The enhanced transparency and disclosure of 'tax-relevant' information are now the new norms of tax administrations world-wide. The demand for increased transparency is reflected in the agendas and action plans of the 'Organisation for Economic Co-operation and Development' (OECD), the G20, the European Union and the United Nations.

The immediate and sweeping initiative in the domain of tax functions is the OECD's 'Country-by-Country Reporting' (CbCR) recommendations and framework. CbCR is expected to make a significant impact on the tax function and how it should engage with the wider business world in order to be ready for compliance related requirements, meet recurring annual tax obligations and respond to information-powered tax administrations in several countries.

Sharing of tax-related information among countries has become the norm, and a large number of Tax Information Exchange Agreements have been signed by India in the last couple of years. Several countries are now looking forward to implementing the 'Base Erosion & Profit Shifting' (BEPS) Action Plans, which have been designed on an assumption of transparency on taxpayers across tax administrations in various countries, and some are planning to make tax data-sharing an automated process.

India has been active in leading OECD member countries on the BEPS initiative and has also been an early adopter of automatic exchange of information.

The Finance Bill 2020 has proposed several crucial and significant amendments and rationalisation measures in the International Taxation arena, which are being discussed as under:

16.1 Exempting Non-Residents from Filing of Income-tax return in certain conditions.

Section 115A of the Act provides for the determination of tax for a non-resident whose total income consists of:

(a)   certain dividend or interest income;

(b)   royalty or fees for technical services (FTS) received from the Government or Indian concern in pursuance of an agreement made after 31st March 1976, and which is not effectively connected with a PE, if any, of the non-resident in India.

Sub-section (5) of said section provides that a non-resident is not required to furnish its return of income under sub-section (1) of section 139 of the Act, if its total income, consists only of certain dividend or interest income and the TDS on such income has been deducted according to the provisions of Chapter XVII-B of the Act.

While, the current provisions of section 115A of the Act provide relief to non-residents from filing of return of income where the non-resident is not liable to pay tax other than the TDS which has been deducted on the dividend or interest income, the same relief has not been extended to non-residents whose total income consists only of the income by way of royalty or FTS of the nature as mentioned in point (b) above. Representations have been received to extend this benefit to royalty and FTS income as well.

Therefore, it has been proposed in the Finance Bill 2020 to amend section 115A of the Act in order to provide that a non-resident, shall not be required to file return of income under sub-section (1) of section 139 of the Act if, -

(i)   his or its total income consists of only dividend or interest income as referred to in clause (a) of sub-section (1) of said section, or royalty or FTS income of the nature specified in clause (b) of sub-section (1) of section 115A; and

(ii)   the TDS on such income has been deducted under the provisions of Chapter XVII-B of the Act at the rates which are not lower than the prescribed rates under sub-section (1) of section 115A.

This amendment will take effect from 1st April, 2020 and will, accordingly, apply in relation to the AY 2020-21 and subsequent assessment years.

16.2 Amendment for providing attribution of profit to Permanent Establishment in Safe Harbour Rules under section 92CB and in Advance Pricing Agreement under section 92CC

Section 92CB of the Act empowers the Central Board of Direct Taxes (Board) for making safe harbour rules (SHR) to which the determination of the arm's length price (ALP) under section 92C or section 92CA of the Act shall be subject to.

As per Explanation to said section the term "safe harbour" means circumstances in which the Income-tax Authority shall accept the transfer price declared by the assessee. This section was inserted in the Act to reduce the number of transfer pricing audits and prolonged disputes especially in case of relatively smaller assessees. Besides reduction of disputes, the SHR provides certainty as well.

Further, section 92CC of the Act empowers the Board to enter into an advance pricing agreement (APA) with any person, determining the ALP or specifying the manner in which the ALP is to be determined, in relation to an international transaction to be entered into by that person. APA provides tax certainty in determination of ALP for five future years as well as for four earlier years (Rollback).

SHR provides tax certainty for relatively smaller cases for future years on general terms, while APA provides tax certainty on case to case basis not only for future years but also Rollback years. Both SHR and the APA have been successful in reducing litigation in determination of the ALP.

It has been represented that the attribution of profits to the PE of a non-resident under clause (i) of sub-section (1) of section 9 of the Act in accordance with rule 10 of the Rules also results in avoidable disputes in a number of cases. In order to provide certainty, the attribution of income in case of a non-resident person to the PE is also required to be clearly covered under the provisions of the SHR and the APA.

In view of the above, it has been proposed in the Finance Bill 2020 to amend section 92CB and section 92CC of the Act to cover determination of attribution to PE within the scope of SHR and APA.

With respect to section 92CB, the amendment will take effect from 1st April, 2020 and will, accordingly, apply in relation to the AY 2020-21 and subsequent assessment years.

With respect to section 92CC, the amendment will take effect from 1st April, 2020 and therefore will apply to an APA entered into on or after 1st April, 2020.

16.3 Deferring Significant Economic Presence (SEP) Proposal

Section 9 of the Act contains provisions in respect of income which are deemed to accrue or arise in India. Sub-section (1) thereof creates a legal fiction that certain incomes shall be deemed to accrue or arise in India.

Clause (i) of sub-section (1) deems the following income to accrue or arise in India:

"all income accruing or arising, whether directly or indirectly, through or from any business connection in India, or through or from any property in India, or through or from any asset or source of income in India, or through the transfer of a capital asset situate in India."

Finance Act, 2018, *inter alia*, inserted Explanation 2A to said clause so as to clarify that the "significant economic presence" (SEP) of a non-resident in India shall constitute "business connection" in India and SEP for this purpose, shall mean:

(a) transaction in respect of any goods, services or property carried out by a non-resident in India including provision of download of data or software in India, if the aggregate of payments arising from such transaction or transactions during the previous year exceeds such amount as may be prescribed; or

(b) systematic and continuous soliciting of business activities or engaging in interaction with such number of users as may be prescribed, in India through digital means.

The said Explanation further provided that the transactions or activities shall constitute significant economic presence in India, whether or not, the agreement for such transactions or activities is entered in India; or the non-resident has a residence or place of business in India; or the non-resident renders services in India. It was also provided that only so much of income as is attributable to the transactions or activities mentioned at para 2(a) and (b) shall be deemed to accrue or arise in India.

Therefore, for the purposes of determining SEP of a non-resident in India, threshold for the aggregate amount of payments arising from the specified transactions and for the number of users were required to be prescribed in the Rules. However, since discussion on this issue is still going on in G20-OECD BEPS project, these numbers have not been notified yet. G20-OECD report is expected by the end of December 2020. In the circumstances, it is proposed to defer the applicability of SEP to starting from assessment year 2022-23. Certain drafting changes have also been made while deferring the proposal.

The current SEP provisions shall be omitted from assessment year 2021-22 and the new provisions will take effect from 1st April, 2022 and will, accordingly, apply in relation to the assessment year 2022-23 and subsequent assessment years.

16.4 Extending Source Rule (Digital Tax)

As per the discussion going on in international forum, countries generally agree that income from advertisement that targets Indian customers or income from sale of data collected from India or income from sale of goods and services using such data collected from India, needs to be accounted for in Indian revenue. Hence, it is proposed to amend the source rule to clarify this position.

This amendment will take effect from 1st April, 2021 and will, accordingly, apply in relation to the AY 2021-22 and subsequent assessment years. However, for attribution of income related to SEP transaction or activities the amendment will take effect from 1st

April, 2022 and will, accordingly, apply in relation to the AY 2022-23 and subsequent assessment years.

16.5 Aligning exemption from taxability of Foreign Portfolio Investors (FPIs), on account of indirect transfer of assets, with amended scheme of SEBI

The Finance Act, 2012, *inter alia*, had inserted Explanation 5 to section 9(1)(v) to clarify that an asset or capital asset being any share or interest in a company or entity registered or incorporated outside India shall be deemed to be and shall always be deemed to have been situated in India if the share or interest derives, directly or indirectly, its value substantially from the assets located in India. Second proviso to said Explanation, inserted through the Finance Act, 2017, provides that the Explanation shall not apply to an asset or capital asset, which is held by a non-resident by way of investment, directly or indirectly, in Category-I or Category-II foreign portfolio investor under the Securities and Exchange Board of India (Foreign Portfolio Investors) Regulations, 2014 [SEBI (FPI) Regulations, 2014].

Vide Gazette Notification No. SEBI/LAD-NRO/GN/2019/36, SEBI has notified Securities and Exchange Board of India (Foreign Portfolio Investors) Regulations, 2019 [SEBI (FPI) Regulations,

2019] and repealed the SEBI (FPI) Regulations, 2014. The difference between these two regulations pertinent in the present context is that the SEBI has done away with the broad basing criteria for the purposes of categorization of portfolios and has reduced the categories from three to two. In view of the same, necessary modification needs to be made in the proviso so inserted. Hence, it is proposed that the exception from said Explanation 5 provided to an asset or a capital asset, held by a non-resident by way of investment in erstwhile Category I and II FPIs under the SEBI (FPI) Regulations, 2014 may be grandfathered. Further, similar exception may be provided in respect of investment in Category-I FPI under the SEBI (FPI) Regulations, 2019.

These amendments will take effect from 1st April, 2020 and will, accordingly, apply in relation to the AY 2020-21 and subsequent assessment years.

16.6 Rationalisation of the definition of Royalty

Clause (vi) of sub-section (1) of section 9 deems certain income by way of royalty to accrue or arise in India. Explanation 2 of said clause defines the term "royalty" to, inter alia, mean the transfer of all or any rights (including the granting of a license) in respect of any copyright, literary, artistic or scientific work including films or video tapes for use in connection with television or tapes for use in connection with radio broadcasting, but not including consideration for the sale, distribution or exhibition of cinematographic films.

Due to exclusion of consideration for the sale, distribution or exhibition of cinematographic films from the definition of royalty, such royalty is not taxable in India even if the DTAA gives India the right to tax such royalty. Such a situation is discriminatory against Indian residents, since India is foregoing its right to tax royalty in case of a non-resident from another country without that other country offering similar concession to Indian resident. Hence, it is proposed to amend the definition of royalty so as not to exclude consideration for the sale, distribution or exhibition of cinematographic films from its meaning.

These amendments will take effect from 1st April, 2021 and will, accordingly, apply in relation to the AY 2021-22 and subsequent assessment years.

It is further proposed to amend section 295 of the Act so as to empower the Board for making rules to provide for the manner in which and the procedure by which the income shall be arrived at in the case of-

(i) operations carried out in India by a non-resident; and

(ii) transaction or activities of a non-resident.

The amendment at clause (i) will take effect from 1st April, 2021 and will, accordingly, apply in relation to the AY 2021-22 and subsequent assessment years. The amendment at clause (ii) will take effect from 1st April, 2022 and will, accordingly, apply in relation to the AY 2022-23 and subsequent assessment years.

16.7 Aligning purpose of entering into Double Taxation Avoidance Agreements (DTAA) with Multilateral Instrument (MLI)

Section 90 of the Act empowers the Central Government to enter into agreement with foreign countries or specified territories (commonly known as DTAAs) for-

(a) granting relief in respect of —

(i) income on which tax has been paid both, in India and that foreign country or territory, or

(ii) income-tax chargeable under the laws of both, India and

that foreign country or territory, to promote mutual economic relations, trade and investment.

(b) avoidance of double taxation of income under the laws of both, India and that foreign country of territory,

(c) exchange of information for prevention of evasion or avoidance of income-tax chargeable under the laws of both India and that foreign country or territory, or investigation of cases of such evasion or avoidance, or

(d) recovery of income-tax under the laws of both India and that foreign country or territory.

Section 90A of the Act contains provision similar to section 90 of the Act so as to empower the Central Government to adopt and implement an agreement between a specified association in India and any specified association in specified territory outside India for granting relief, avoidance of double taxation, exchange of information and recovery of income-tax.

India has signed the Multilateral Convention to Implement Tax Treaty Related Measures to Prevent Base Erosion and Profit Shifting (commonly referred to as MLI) along with representatives of many countries, which has since been ratified. India has since deposited the Instrument of Ratification to OECD, Paris along with its Final Position in terms of Covered Tax Agreements (CTAs), Reservations, Options and Notifications under the MLI, as a result of which MLI has entered into force for India on 1st October, 2019 and its provisions will be applicable on India's DTAAs from FY 2020-21 onwards.

The MLI is an outcome of the G20-OECD project to tackle Base Erosion and Profit Shifting (the BEPS Project), i.e. tax planning strategies that exploit gaps and mismatches in tax rules to artificially shift profits to low or no-tax locations where there is little or no economic activity, resulting in little or no overall corporate tax being paid. The MLI will modify India's DTAAs to curb revenue loss through treaty abuse and base erosion and profit shifting strategies by ensuring that profits are taxed where substantive economic activities generating the profits are carried out. The MLI will be applied alongside existing DTAAs, modifying their application in order to implement the BEPS measures.

Article 6 of MLI provides for modification of the Covered Tax Agreement to include the following preamble text:

"Intending to eliminate double taxation with respect to the taxes covered by this agreement without creating opportunities for non-taxation or reduced taxation through tax evasion or avoidance (including through treaty-shopping arrangements aimed at obtaining reliefs provided in this agreement for the indirect benefit of residents of third jurisdictions),"

In order to achieve this, clause (b) of sub-section (1) of section 90 of the Act which provides for providing relief in respect of avoidance of double taxation of income under the laws of both country or territory (India and the other foreign country of territory) is required to contain the text provided for in MLI as mentioned at para 4 above. In case of section 90A of the Act also, similar amendment would be required to be carried out.

Therefore, it is proposed to amend clause (b) of sub-section (1) of section 90 of the Act so as to provide that the Central Government may enter into an agreement with the Government of any country outside India or specified territory outside India for, inter alia, the avoidance of double taxation of income under the Act and under the corresponding law in force in that country or specified territory, as the case may be, without creating opportunities for non-taxation or reduced taxation through tax evasion or avoidance (including through treaty-shopping arrangements aimed at obtaining reliefs provided in this agreement for the indirect benefit of residents of any other country or territory).

It is also proposed to make similar amendment in clause (b) of sub-section (1) of section 90A of the Act.

These amendments will take effect from 1st April, 2021 and will, accordingly, apply in relation to the AY 2021-22 and subsequent assessment years.

Chapter 17

Miscellaneous Amendments

17. In our previous Chapters, we have discussed and understood in detail the nuances and nitty-gritties of all major and significant amendments and provisions as proposed in the Finance Bill 2020.

In this Chapter, the remaining miscellaneous but important proposed amendments are being discussed and explained in detail as under:

17.1 Deeming Residential Status of a Person of Indian Origin or an Indian Citizen, who is not liable to tax in any other country or territory.

By virtue of the existing provisions of section 6(1) read with clause (b) of Explanation 1 of said section provides that an individual who is an Indian Citizen or a person of Indian Origin, shall be Indian resident in a year, if he-

(i) has been in India for an overall period of 365 days or more within four years preceding that year, and

(ii) is in India for an overall period of 182 days or more in that year.

In order or to prevent the perceived misuse of this provision, wherein an Individual being an Indian citizen or a person of Indian origin, carrying out substantial economic activities from India, manages the period of his stay in India for less than 182 days, so as to remain a non-resident in perpetuity and not be required to declare his global income in India, it has been proposed in the Finance Bill 2020, that-

(i) the exception provided in clause (b) of Explanation 1 of sub-section (1) to section 6 for visiting India in that year be decreased to 120 days from existing 182 days.

(ii) an individual or an HUF shall be said to be "not ordinarily resident" in India in a previous year, if the individual or the manager of the HUF has been a non-resident in India in seven out of ten previous years preceding that year. This new condition to replace the existing conditions in clauses (a) and (b) of sub-section (6) of section 6.

(iii) an Indian citizen who is not liable to tax in any other country or territory shall be deemed to be resident in India.

This amendment will take effect from 1st April, 2021 and will, accordingly, apply in relation to the assessment year 2021-22 and subsequent assessment years.

Therefore, w.e.f. AY 2021-22, an Indian Citizen or a Person of Indian Origin, who is not liable to tax in any other country or territory even on account of operation of different tax treaties or tax-heaven status of the countries of his stay, will be deemed to be the resident person of India, and accordingly will be taxed on his global income, in India.

17.2 Insertion of Taxpayer's Charter in the Act

In the Finance Bill 2020, it has been proposed to insert a new section 119A in the Act to empower the CBDT Board to adopt and declare a Taxpayer's Charter and issue such orders, instructions, directions or guidelines to other income-tax authorities as it may deem fit for the administration of Charter.

This amendment will take effect from 1st April, 2020.

17.3 Amendment in the provisions of Act relating to verification of the return of income and appearance of authorized representative.

Section 140 of the Act provides that in case of company the return is required to be verified by the managing director (MD) thereof. Where the MD is not able to verify for any unavoidable reason or where there is no MD, any director of the company can verify the return. It is also provided that in case of a company in whose case application for insolvency resolution process has been admitted by the Adjudicating Authority (AA) under the Insolvency and Bankruptcy Code, 2016 (IBC), the return has to be verified by the insolvency professional appointed by such AA. Similarly, in case of a limited liability partnership (LLP), the return has to be verified by the designated partner of the LLP or by any partner, in case there is no such designated partner.

Therefore, it has been proposed in the Finance Bill 2020, to amend clause (c) and (cd) of section 140 of the Act so as to enable any other person, as may be prescribed by the Board to verify the return of income in the cases of a company and a limited liability partnership.

Further, section 288 of the Act provides for the persons entitled to appear before any Income-tax Authority or the Appellate Tribunal, on behalf of an assessee, as its "authorised representative", in connection with any proceedings under that Act. While the IBC empowers the Insolvency Professional or the Administrator to exercise the powers of the Board of Directors or corporate debtor, it has been reported that lack of explicit reference in section 288 of the Act for an Insolvency Professional to act as an authorised representative of the corporate debtor has been raising certain practical difficulties.

Therefore, it is proposed to amend sub-section (2) of section 288 to enable any other person, as may be prescribed by the Board, to appear as an authorised representative.

These amendments will take effect from 1st April, 2020.

17.4 Providing Check on Survey Operations under section 133A of the Act.

Under the existing provisions of section 133A of the Act, an income-tax authority as defined therein is empowered to conduct survey at the business premises of the assessee under his jurisdiction. To prevent the possible misuse of such powers, vide

Finance Act 2003, a proviso to sub-section (6) in the said section was inserted to provide that no income-tax authority below the rank of Joint Director or Joint Commissioner, shall conduct any survey under the said section without prior approval of the Joint Director or the Joint Commissioner, as the case may be.

It has been proposed to substitute the proviso to sub-section (6) of section 133A to provide that-

(A) in a case where the information has been received from the prescribed authority, no income-tax authority below the rank of Joint Director or Joint Commissioner, shall conduct any survey under the said section without prior approval of the Joint Director or the Joint Commissioner, as the case may be; and

(B) in any other case, no income-tax authority below the rank of Commissioner or Director, shall conduct any survey under the said section without prior approval of the Commissioner or the Director, as the case may be.

This amendment will take effect from 1st April, 2020.

17.5 Amendment in Dispute Resolution Panel (DRP)

Section 144C of the Act provides that in case of certain eligible assessees, viz., foreign companies and any person in whose case transfer pricing adjustments have been made under sub-section (3) of section 92CA of the Act, the Assessing Officer (AO) is required to forward a draft assessment order to the eligible assessee, if he proposes to make any variation in the income or loss returned which is prejudicial to the interest of such assessee. Such eligible assessee with respect to such variation may file his objection to the DRP, a collegium of three Principal Commissioners or Commissioners of Income-tax. DRP has nine months to pass directions which are binding on the AO.

It is proposed that the provisions of section 144C of the Act may be suitably amended to:

(A) include cases, where the AO proposes to make any variation which is prejudicial to the interest of the assessee, within the ambit of section 144C;

(B) expand the scope of the said section by defining eligible assessee as a non-resident not being a company, or a foreign company.

This amendment will take effect from 1st April, 2020. Thus, if the AO proposes to make any variation after this date, in case of eligible assessee, which is prejudicial to the interest of the assessee, the above provision shall be applicable.

17.6 Amendment of section 115BAB of the Act to include generation of electricity as manufacturing.

The Taxation Laws (Amendment) Act 2019, (TLAA), *inter-alia*, inserted section 115BAB in the Act. The newly inserted section provides that new manufacturing domestic companies set up on or after 1st October, 2019, which commence manufacturing or production by 31st March, 2023 and do not avail of any specified incentives or deductions, may opt to pay tax at a concessional rate of 15 per cent. Further, Explanation to clause (b) of sub-section (2) thereof provides that for the purposes of the said section, businesses engaged in development of computer software, mining, conversion of marble blocks or similar items into slabs, bottling of gas into cylinder, printing of books or production of cinematograph film or any other business as may be notified by the Central

Government will not be considered as manufacturing or production.

Representations have been received from various stakeholders requesting to provide that the benefit of the concessional rate under section 115BAB of the Act may also be extended to business of generation of electricity, which otherwise may not amount to manufacturing or production of an article or thing. Accordingly, it is proposed to explain that, for the purposes of this section, manufacturing or production of an article or thing shall include generation of electricity.

This amendment will take effect from 1st April, 2020 and will, accordingly, apply in relation to the AY 2020-21 and subsequent assessment years.

17.7 Incentives to Affordable Housing Sector

a. Extending time limit for approval of affordable housing project for availing deduction under section 80-IBA of the Act.

The existing provisions of section 80-IBA of the Act, *inter alia*, provide that where the gross total income of an assessee includes any profits and gains derived from the business of developing and building affordable housing projects, there shall, subject to certain conditions specified therein, be allowed a deduction of an amount equal to one hundred per cent of the profits and gains derived from such business. The conditions contained in the section, inter alia, prescribe that the project is approved by the competent authority during the period from 1st June, 2016 to 31st March, 2020.

In order to incentivise building affordable housing to boost the supply of such houses, the period of approval of the project by the competent authority is proposed to be extended to 31st March, 2021.

This amendment will take effect from 1st April, 2021 and will, accordingly, apply in relation to the AY 2021-22 and subsequent assessment years.

b. Extending time limit for sanctioning of loan for affordable housing for availing deduction under section 80EEA of the Act

The existing provisions of section 80EEA of the Act provide for a deduction in respect of interest on loan taken from any financial institution for acquisition of an affordable residential house property. The deduction allowed is up to one lakh fifty thousand rupees and is subject to certain conditions. One of the conditions is that loan has been sanctioned by the financial institution during the period from 1st April, 2019 to 31st March, 2020.

The said deduction is aimed to incentivise first time buyers to invest in residential house property whose stamp duty does not exceed forty-five lakh rupees. In order to continue promoting purchase of affordable housing, the period of sanctioning of loan by the financial institution is proposed to be extended to 31st March, 2021.

This amendment will take effect from 1st April, 2021 and will, accordingly, apply in relation to the AY 2021-22 and subsequent assessment years.

Chapter 18

Post Budget Bucket List of "BUSINESS" from the Finance Minister

"Hi Friends!!

I am 'Business'.

In India, I exist in different forms and structures. I may be carried out by a proprietory concern, a partnership firm, LLP or a corporate entity. I play a vital and crucial role in accelerating the growth rate in the current sluggish economy. I have the potential for the much-needed revival of the slowing economy by making investments in core infrastructure facilities and sectors and generating substantial employment opportunities and thereby increasing the per capita income of the end consumers to augment the much-needed consumption.

If given a conducive and friendly environment to flourish, I have the capacity and the capability to do all this, on my own. But now, as they say, *'Milk'* also requires the help of *'Complan'* to increase its nutritive power, similarly I also require the assistance and support of the Government and the Finance Ministry in the upcoming Union Budget 2020, so as to give me the requisite push and fillip.

Our FM Smt. Nirmala Sitharaman has been kind, generous, sensitive and responsive enough to seek the post-budget feedbacks and suggestions for further rationalisation of the Union Budget/Finance Bill 2020, from all the stakeholders concerned.

So, being one of the biggest stakeholders, I am sharing below, my post-budget memorandum or the 'bucket-list', in my various forms.

Hope, the Finance Minister is listening….

(I) **Corporate Business Entities:**

(i) Relaxation in the provisions of newly inserted section 115BAA and 115BAB concerning restrictions on the availment of specified deductions and allowances for reduced corporate tax rate of 22% / 15%, respectively.

The Taxation Laws (Amendment) Act 2019, has brought good news for me, by way of introduction of two new sections viz. section 115BAA and section 115BAB providing for reduced taxation regimes, whereby corporate tax rates have been reduced to 15% and 22% in case of newly incorporated domestic manufacturing companies and non-manufacturing companies, respectively w.e.f. 1.10.2019.

Under the newly inserted section 115BAA, a domestic company has an option to pay tax at the reduced rate of 22% provided it does not claim specified deductions, allowances and brought forward MAT credit and unabsorbed accelerated/additional depreciation.

Thus, a domestic corporate entity has to do a trade-off between the reduced tax rate of 22% vis-à-vis the availment of specified deductions, allowances and brought-forward MAT credit and unabsorbed accelerated/additional depreciation, which in a way is diluting the benefit of reduced tax rate.

So, it is my wish and request that this conditional benefit of the reduced tax rate, should be relaxed and the domestic corporate entity opting for the reduced tax rate of 22%, should be allowed to adjust its unabsorbed business losses on account of unabsorbed additional depreciation and the MAT credit, if any, from its income of the previous year, in which the option of reduced tax rate has been exercised. Such restrictions concerning the non-availment of specified deductions, allowances and brought-forward MAT credit and unabsorbed accelerated/additional depreciation may be imposed for subsequent assessment years.

Further, it is my desire and wish that the scope of section 115BAB of the Income Tax Act, providing for the reduced tax rate of 15% in case of newly incorporated domestic manufacturing companies w.e.f. 1.10.2019, may be enlarged so as to include the job-work and ancillary activities also within the purview of manufacturing activities so as to qualify for the reduced tax rate.

(ii) Start-Ups:

With a view to encourage and promote 'my nascent stage' more popularly known as 'Start-ups', several incentives and amendments have been proposed in the Finance Bill 2020 (which have been discussed in detail in Chapter No. 9).

However, there is a need to further rationalise and streamline the legislative provisions concerning Start-Ups', as under:

(a) Angel Tax: Non-applicability of the provisions of section 56(2)(viib)/56(2)(x) on Eligible Start-ups u/s 80IAC of the Act:

The CBDT as per its Circular No. 22/2019 dated 30.8.2019, has stipulated the specified procedure in ongoing assessments of 'eligible start-ups' whose cases are under limited scrutiny on the single issue of applicability of section 56(2)(viib) and has provided that the contentions of such 'start-ups' in this regard, shall be summarily accepted.

However, in order to avoid any uncertainty and confusion in this regards, an express and specific amendment in section 56(2)(viib)/56(2)(x) of the Act, concerning the non-applicability of the provisions of these sections to the eligible start-up entities u/s 80IAC of the Act, is desired and required.

(b) Relaxation in the provisions of Section 79 concerning carry-forward and set-off of losses:

The Finance Act 2017 has amended section 79 to provide that in the cases of eligible start-ups u/s 80IAC of the Act, where a change in shareholding has taken place in a previous year, loss shall be allowed to be carried forward and set-off against the income of such previous year, only if all the shareholders of such company carrying voting rights, on the last day of the year in which the loss was incurred, continue to hold those shares on the last day of such previous year. This condition of continuity of the shareholding is causing practical difficulties for the 'start-ups' as PE investors in the 'start-ups' generally look at the time frame of 3-5 years for exit at a higher price. So, any such exit will trigger section 79 limitation, for the 'start-up'.

In view of the practical difficulties and realistic considerations, this condition of continuity of 100% shareholding of the promoters/investors of the 'start-ups' u/s 79 may be relaxed and instead an appropriate percentage say 20% or 25% may be specified, for operational flexibility.

(iii) Relaxation in the applicability of provisions concerning fair market valuation of shares u/s 56(2)(viia)/56(2)(x) of the Income Tax Act in the cases of fresh issuance of shares/bonus issue/right issue and buy back of shares by companies:

Central Board of Direct Taxes had issued Circular No. 10/2018 dated 31.12.2018 to clarify that provisions of section 56(2)(viia) of the Income-tax Act, 1961 being anti-abuse provisions shall not be applicable in cases of receipt of shares by the specified company or firm as a result of fresh issuance of shares including by way of bonus shares, rights shares and preference shares or transactions of similar nature by the specified company. However, on reconsideration it was found that the matter relating to interpretation of the term 'receives' used in section 56(2)(viia) of the act is pending before judicial forums and stakeholders have sought clarifications on other similar

203

provisions in section 56 of the Act. Accordingly, with the idea of issuing a fresh comprehensive circular on the subject, the circular no. 10/2018 was withdrawn by circular no. 02/2019 dated 04.01.2019. While withdrawing the circular no. 10/2018, it was also clarified that the said circular shall be considered to have never been issued.

Subsequently, it was clarified vide circular no. 3/2019 dated 21.01.2019 that the view, taken in circular no. 10/2018 (subsequently withdrawn by circular no. 02/2019) that section 56(2)(viia) of the Act would not apply to fresh issuance of shares, would not be a correct approach, as it could be subject to abuse and would be contrary to the express provisions and the legislative intent of section 56(2)(viia) or similar provisions contained in section 56(2) of the Act. Accordingly, it was further clarified that any view expressed by the Board in Circular No. 10/2018 shall be considered to have never been expressed and, the said circular shall not be taken into account by any Income-tax authority in any proceedings under the Act.

Ironically, the view expressed in CBDT Circular No. 10/2018 dated 31.12.2018 concerning the non-applicability of provisions of section 56(2)(viia) {now amended as section 56(2)(x)} of the Income Tax Act, in cases of receipt of shares by the specified company or firm as a result of fresh issuance of shares including by way of bonus shares, rights shares and preference shares or transactions of similar nature, was in complete harmony and conformity with the legislative intent of introduction of the said anti-abuse provision of section 56(2)(viia) by the Finance Act 2010.

The Explanatory Memorandum to Finance Bill 2010 explaining the rationale of introduction of the said section 56(2)(viia), interalia provided that,

"In order to prevent the practice of transferring unlisted shares at prices much below their market value, it is proposed to amend Section 56(2) to also include within its ambit, transactions undertaken in shares of a company (not being a company in which public are substantially interested) either for inadequate consideration or without consideration where recipient is a Firm or a Company"

Thus it is amply clear and duly evident from above that the legislative intent of introduction of section 56(2)(viia) was to prevent the practice of **transferring** unlisted shares at prices below their fair market value. The expression "transfer" has altogether different connotation and meaning than the expression "issuance" and as such the provisions of said section 56(2)(viia) were meant to be applicable in cases of receipt of shares by a company or a firm on subsequent transfer of unlisted shares after their initial issuance by the issuing company.

Therefore, in view of the above stated legislative intent of introduction of section 56(2)(viia) and in order to give the much needed flexibility to the corporate sector in raising its capital for its genuine financial needs, a suitable amendment either by way of insertion of an explanation or a proviso in now applicable section 56(2)(x) to the effect that provisions of the said section are applicable only in cases of receipt of shares as a result of transfer of such shares and are not to be made applicable in cases of receipt of shares by the specified company or firm as a result of fresh issuance of shares including by way of bonus shares, rights shares and preference shares or transactions of similar nature, is requested to be made in the upcoming Finance Bill 2020.

(iv) Stressed/Insolvent Companies under Insolvency & Bankruptcy Code (IBC) Amendment Act 2019:

As per our conditioning, we naturally take extra care of those body parts in our human body, which have become sick. Similarly, in my case also, those stressed/insolvent companies under IBC 2016, wherein resolution plans for my revival are under consideration by NCLT, extra care, concern and more responsive and sensitive approach is desired by the Law-makers.

(a) Suitable Amendment to ensure Non-Applicability of the provisions of section 56(2)(x) & 50CA to the insolvent companies whose resolution plans for their revival have been approved by NCLT under IBC Amendment Act 2019:

The repealing of the erstwhile SICA Act and its substitution with the new Insolvency & Bankruptcy Code (IBC) 2016, is being considered as a path-breaking initiative of the Central Government. The new IBC Act 2016 is more holistic and sensitive in its approach to ensure more effective financial revival of the insolvent companies as well as protecting the interests of all stakeholders & financial & operational creditors.

Thus, it becomes all the more important and crucial to incentivize and boost the potential buyers/bidders to encourage them to come out with effective resolution plans under IBC. However, potential buyers/bidders desirous of acquiring insolvent companies face the bottlenecks of tax authorities challenging the valuation aspects of the acquisition under section 50CA and 56(2)(x) of the Income Tax Act.

Under Sections 50CA and 56(2)(x) of the Income Tax Act, the differential between the fair market value and the bidding consideration is taxable if the bidding consideration is lower than the fair market value. Section 50CA imposes a tax on this notional capital gain income on the seller and Section 56(2)(x) imposes a tax on the buyer by treating the difference as income from other sources.

The FMV of the securities has to be calculated as per the Rule 11UA of the Income Tax Rules, 1962 with book value or stock market prices to be taken into account. There may be situations, where the bid price of these securities is lower than the FMV determined under Rule 11UA. Since these transactions of bidding are being undertaken in the open market through a competitive bidding process, it would be grossly unfair to tax the sellers and buyers on this notional income.

Since the government has identified the success of IBC as a key determinant of economic growth, it is therefore imperative for the concerned finance ministry and revenue authorities to have a more compassionate and rational view as far as taxing such strategic acquisitions of insolvent companies under IBC.

Thus, in order to augment the success of such a noble initiative of IBC 2016, suitable amendments in section 56(2)(x) & 50CA are requested to be made in the Finance Bill 2020, so as to make them inapplicable on such insolvent companies whose resolution plans for their financial revival have been approved by NCLT under IBC Act 2016.

(b)Amendment in sections 28(iv) & 41(1) to ensure non taxability of the waiver of loans/liabilities of the insolvent companies under IBC Amendment Act 2019:

The waiver of loans and liabilities of the insolvent companies by the financial and operational creditors form an integral part of all the resolution plans aimed at financial revival of insolvent companies under IBC 2016.

Recently the Hon'ble Supreme Court in the case of *Mahindra and Mahindra Ltd.* [2018] 93 taxmann.com 32 (SC), has laid down the law that waiver of loan shall not be taxable either u/s 28(iv) or s.41(1).

The Apex court has now clarified that 'waiver of loan' should be treated as 'receipt of money' and hence such receipt of money would fall outside the purview of s.28(iv) and accordingly cannot be taxable.

The Apex Court has also held that 'waiver of loan' does not amount to cessation of trading liability and as such the same would not fall within the purview of s.41(1).

Therefore, in view of the binding nature of the above judgement of the Hon'ble Supreme Court and more importantly in order to provide the much needed boost and push to IBC 2016 aimed at ensuring financial revival of insolvent companies, suitable amendments in section 28(iv) and 41(1) of the Income Tax Act are requested to be made so as to ensure their non-applicability to the waiver of loans and liabilities of insolvent companies under IBC 2016.

Similar amendments are requested to be made under MAT provision u/s 115JB so as to ensure non-inclusion of such waiver of loans and liabilities in book profits of insolvent companies under IBC, for the purpose of MAT determination.

(c) **Relaxation in provisions of section 2(1B), 2(19AA) & 72A of the Act concerning allowability of carry forward and setoff of losses and unabsorbed depreciation in case of insolvent companies under IBC Act 2016:**

In making strategic acquisitions of insolvent companies under IBC 2016, the consideration of income tax benefit of availment of set-off benefit towards brought-forward business losses and unabsorbed depreciation of insolvent companies plays a very significant role in luring the potential bidders/buyers and it is a universal phenomenon in almost all strategic business acquisitions under IBC 2016.

The conditions for availing the benefit of set-off towards brought-forward business losses and unabsorbed depreciation of the amalgamating/demerging entity is stipulated in section 72A of the Act within the meaning of section 2(1B) or 2(19AA) of the Act.

The primary conditions as envisaged in section 72A are that atleast 75% of the shareholders of the amalgamating/demerging entity must be given shareholding in the amalgamated/demerged entity, amalgamated/demerged company must hold at least 75% of the book value of fixed assets of the amalgamating/demerging entity for a minimum period of five years from the date of amalgamation/demerger; and that the new entity must continue the business of the stressed company for a minimum period of five years from the date of amalgamation/demerger. If either of the conditions is not met, the tax benefit of loss and depreciation is to be taxed in the year the condition is breached.

All these conditions, may in a certain type of resolution plans, be difficult to comply with. Plans which require significant divestment of fixed assets for reasons of business viability may be hit by this embargo. The limitation on the continuation of the old business after amalgamation hampers the flexibility of the acquirer to bring about a turnaround by restructuring the old business into a new business which is viable. In such situations, acquirers/bidders would be hampered by not being able to take the amalgamation route.

In view of above, suitable relaxations in section 2(1B), 2(19AA) and section 72A of the Act are requested to be made in the Finance Bill 2020, so as to make them inapplicable on insolvent companies under IBC 2016, so as to encourage more potential buyers and bidders to participate in the resolution plans for ensuring the financial revival of such insolvent companies.

(v) Incorporating time bound limitation period for issuing income tax refunds in the Income Tax Act:

Delay in processing of income tax refunds of assessees and business enterprises has become a recurring and universal phenomenon. In order to meet out the budgetary targets of demand, refunds are being withheld for no justifiable reasons.

Currently apart from the nominal compensatory interest for delay in refund, there is no other provision in the Income Tax Act stipulating any limitation period for issuing refunds. In view of the Governments' objective of ensuring "ease of doing business" and the CBDT's goal of ensuring taxpayer friendly regime, suitable provisions must be incorporated in the Income Tax Act itself to incorporate time bound limitation periods for issuing refunds and fixing accountability for delays beyond that limitation period.

(II) Partnership Firms/LLPs:

In India, apart from corporate entities, I am being carried out by other forms of organisations/entities also like partnership firms and Limited Liability Partnerships (LLPs).

There should not be any discrimination on the basis of my form and structure and as such the benefit of reduced tax rate of 15% and 22%, available only to corporate entities at present, should also be extended to my all other forms and structures including partnership firms and LLPs.

(III) Proprietory Concerns:

In line with the new regime of reduced corporate tax rates, introduced by the Taxation Laws

(Amendment) Act 2019, the Finance Bill 2020, has proposed the **insertion of a new section 115BAC**, providing for a new personal taxation regime in the cases of individuals and HUFs (hereinafter referred to as 'assessees'), wherein the 'assessees' have been given the option to either continue with the existing personal tax rates with availment of full specified deductions, or to opt for the new regime of reduced personal tax rates with restrictions on approximately 70% of the specified deductions, currently available to them under different chapters and sections, **which in a way is diluting the benefit of reduced tax rate.**

So, it is my wish and request that this conditional benefit of the reduced tax rate, should be relaxed and the individuals and HUFs assessees opting for the new regime of reduced personal tax rate, should be allowed to avail the specified deductions which are required to be foregone, in order to avail the benefit of reduced tax rates.

Such restrictions concerning the non-availment of specified deductions, allowances and brought-forward unabsorbed accelerated/additional depreciation may be imposed after a gestation period of 3 years.

Concluding Remarks:

This is yet to be seen as to whether the **'King has actually given back copiously or not'**, but nonetheless, a balanced approach towards accelerating the growth rate of economy via the tax reforms and simultaneously pegging the fiscal deficit to a tolerable range of 3.8% of GDP, which is slightly higher than the figure of 3.3 for the previous fiscal, has been maintained in the Finance Bill 2020.

Before parting, I would like to convey my sincere and heart-felt request to the FM, through my worthy readers, as under:

"Focus and work on 'making me Easy' and not 'making me Busy in unproductive litigations and disputes'",

by incorporating provisions concerning issue of time-bound refunds, and fixing accountability and responsibility of the erring and over-reaching and over-stretching concerned authorities, in the Act itself.

Nonetheless, the positive and growth centric tax rationalisation measures, which have been proposed in the Finance Bill 2020, are welcome and appreciated.

All in all, the Union Budget 2020, is a mixed basket of carrots and sticks, aimed at encouraging voluntary compliance by taxpayers, augmenting tax revenues, widening the tax base and further streamlining of tax administration.

"To be curious is a good thing and to be able to satisfy one's curiosity is even better..."

*****

www.ingramcontent.com/pod-product-compliance
Lightning Source LLC
Chambersburg PA
CBHW030927180526
45163CB00002B/487